D1359596

14.45

REPAIRING
THE BREACH

REPAIRING THE BREACH

Key Ways to Support Family Life,
Reclaim Our Streets,
and Rebuild Civil Society
in America's Communities

Report of the National Task Force
on African-American Men and Boys
ANDREW J. YOUNG, CHAIRMAN

EDITOR:
BOBBY WILLIAM AUSTIN

WRITING COMMITTEE:
Paul Martin DuBois, Jacquelyn Madry-Taylor,
Robert L. Green, George E. Ayers,
Marilyn Melkonian, and Roscoe Ellis

NOBLE PRESS, INC.
Chicago, Illinois

Copyright © 1996 by the W. K. Kellogg Foundation, One Michigan Avenue East, Battle Creek, Michigan 49017-4058. Copyright under international Pan American and Universal copyright conventions. All rights reserved. No part of this book may be reproduced in any form—except for brief quotations (not to exceed 1,000 words) in a review or professional work—without permission in writing from the publishers.

Acknowledgments:

Special thanks to Joy Austin, Des Bracey, Vickie Brown, Debra Hausman, Jean Kline, Johnie Lindhurst and staff, Carolyn Pegram of CRP Inc., Cheri Ruble, and Diana Scales of Scales & Associates for their assistance in preparing this report.

This report was funded by the W. K. Kellogg Foundation of Battle Creek, Michigan. The information and recommendations contained herein do not necessarily reflect the views of the W. K. Kellogg Foundation or its management.

Published by

NOBLE PRESS, INC.
213 W. Institute Place
Chicago, IL 60610

Phone: 312/642-1168

Published by arrangement with Alpine Guild, Inc.

Library of Congress Cataloging-in-Publication Data

National Task Force on African-American Men and Boys.
    Repairing the Breach : key ways to support family
life, reclaim our streets, and rebuild civil society in
America's communities : report of the National Task
Force on African-American Men and Boys.
Andrew Young, chairman / editor, Bobby William
Austin.
        p.   cm.
    Includes bibliographical references and index.
    ISBN 1–879360–45–4
    1. Afro-American men.   2. Afro-American boys.
3. Afro-American families.   4. Community develop-
ment—United States.   5. Social action—United
States.   I. Young, Andrew. 1932–   . II Austin,
Bobby William.   III. Title.
E185.86.N368   1996
305.38′896073—dc20   96–17532
                                                CIP

Table of
CONTENTS

PREFACE:
Public Ideas and Public Work

*T*HE rupture of American public life and discourse is evident everywhere. This report of the National Task Force on African-American Men and Boys is the beginning of an approach to repair society's breaches and restore our streets to safety.

The Task Force has provided information and ideas which organizations and individuals can use to begin transforming communities—and thereby assist boys and their families. We want to create long-term structures for sustained intervention for boys in trouble. We must have systemic change, in which many ideas are brought together, so that crime and violence are reduced and social life is made whole. We each have a part to play.

The Nation

Three concepts were presented to the Task Force. These are concepts the entire nation must discuss.

First, the concept of the Human Condition and Human Development which focuses on the common good and connects human to human. Fair play, expanded opportunities, and the necessity of each person to contribute to society are ideas the nation must discuss.

Second, the concept of polis, signifying here that members of a society have both rights and duties. The rules of law and the etiquette of a community and society must be honored or the nation will pay the consequences.

Third, the concept of Public Work. This concept is defined through the following principles outlined by Dr. Harry Boyte:

a. Public work involves the contributions everyday people make to the commonwealth. It involves non-violence and human dignity. It calls for creativity and individual accountability.

b. Public work means learning to work effectively with people with whom you do not agree or may not even like.

c. Public work involves craft and skills, as well as pride in work. Citizenship is public work that must be developed. No one is born into it.

d. Public work is visible and involves civic storytelling about ordinary people doing extraordinary things for each other and the community.

e. Public work puts experts on tap, not on top. Government officials must see themselves as citizens, working with people, not doing things to or for them. Our institutions must become civic public spaces.

f. Public work means that different groups work together, with focus and seriousness, so that people can hear one another and understand each other's stories of injustice, deprivation, suffering, and oppression.

g. Public work develops, in those people who do it, a sense of self, as well as skills and accountability.

We must rebuild the notion of public work and citizenship or cries for justice will fall on deaf ears. Young men and boys will fail to understand their place in American life and will continue to throw away their futures for jail cells, believing that they are not a part of this significant experience of American democracy.

The Community

From these concepts emerged themes around which this Report is framed. These themes are the keys to strengthening families, restoring our streets to safety, and rebuilding civil societies in communities.

Polis   This theme, building on the concept of polis outlined above, is a comprehensive idea regarding the values, manners, morals, and etiquette needed for restructuring public life. It involves building a sense of community, and an understanding of both rights and responsibilities within the community.

Civic Storytelling   This theme focuses on how these boys and their ancestors fit into American culture. It honors the ordinary citizen who becomes a hero by successfully creating public kinship. The arts, humanities, and education play a role and the civic story is told and retold to establish one's place in society and to create public kinship.

Grassroots Civic Leadership This theme aims to empower individuals to take control of their lives and communities through the development and use of effective leadership skills.

Common Good This theme focuses on creating the common good, using entrepreneurship, economic development, educational reform, and other ideas.

Restoring Community Institutions This theme focuses on reinventing and restructuring civil and social life in communities. It involves housing issues, the development of new philanthropic organizations, and the creation of new ways to deliver multi-focused, multi-purpose programming for boys.

Civic Dialogue This theme stresses that capacity and understanding are built through dialogue which overcomes hate and mistrust.

The work suggested by these themes can be accomplished by the cooperative activities of civic, social, religious, professional, business, governmental, and philanthropic organizations.

The Task Force recommendations involve the short-term in *Project 2000*, to last through the year 2000. They also involve the long-term, a twenty-year *Generation Plan* which will work to implement the recommendations of the Task Force.

Individuals

Individuals, as well as organizations, must join in this multi-faceted effort over many years. A major tool will be a National Conversation/Dialogue on Race. This will help to shape public opinion which is vital for change to occur. This conversation/dialogue will take place over the next several years.

A dialogue within the African-American community will begin in 1996. Task Force members will talk to neighbors, friends, colleagues, and others in homes, town halls, churches, and the work place.

Spiritual Dimension

From these public ideas, concepts, themes, plans, conversations, and dialogues we can heal the breach between
> Sons and Mothers
> Sons and Fathers
> Mothers and Fathers
> Boys and Girls
> Sisters and Brothers
> Fathers and Daughters
> Mothers and Daughters
> Men and Women
> Boys and Community
> Boys and Society
> Blacks and Whites
> and Within Ourselves.

On the back of this book is a quotation from the Book of Isaiah. This quotation was used by Ambassador Andrew Young in a nationally televised sermon. The idea of repairing the breach and restoring the streets to dwell in was taken by the Task Force as a personal challenge as well as an injunction to each citizen of our nation to play a part in bringing wholeness to our fractured and disrupted world.

Boys and Men

In the final analysis, boys and men who are in trouble or are headed toward trouble must decide for themselves that they want to change. They must assume personal responsibility and be held accountable for their own actions.

There are always those who will help. The names of many organizations appear later in this Report. They are doing successful work with men and boys who wish to change and they are helping concerned parents. Throughout the nation, organizations and programs have sprung up—doing things that work!

If each of us joins in to work together, all our futures will be brighter.

PROLOGUE:
The Nation's Problem

*M*ARK, *if you please, the fact, for it is a fact, an ominous fact, that at no time in the history of the conflict between slavery and freedom in this country has the character of the Negro as a man been made the subject of a fiercer and more serious discussion in all the avenues of debate than during the past and present year. Against him have been marshaled the whole artillery of science, philosophy, and history. We are not only controlled by open foes, but we are assailed in the guise of sympathy and friendship and presented as objects of pity.*

The strong point made against him and his cause is the statement, widely circulated and greatly relied upon, that no two people so different in race and color can live together in the same country on a level of equal, civil and political rights, and powers; that nature herself has ordained that the relations of two such races must be that of domination on the one hand and subjugation on the other. This old slaveholding Calhoun and McDuffy doctrine, which we long ago thought dead and buried, is revived in unexpected quarters, and controls us today as sternly and bitterly as it did forty years ago. Then it was employed as a justification of the fraud and violence by which colored men are divested of their citizenship, and robbed of their constitutional rights in the solid South.

The Negro is now a member of the body politic. This talk about him implies that he is regarded as a diseased member. It is wisely said by physicians that any member of the human body is in a healthy condition when it gives no occasion to think of it. The fact that the American people of the Caucasian race are continually thinking of the Negro, and never cease to call attention to him, shows that his relation to them is felt to be abnormal and unhealthy. . . .

I have said that at no time has the character of the Negro been so generally, seriously and unfavorably discussed as now. I do not regard discussion as an evil in itself. On the contrary I regard it not as an enemy, but as a friend. It has served us well at other times in our history, and I hope it may serve us well hereafter. Controversy, whether of words or blows, whether in the forum or on the battle field, may help us, if we but make the right use of it. We are not, however, to be like dumb driven cattle in this discussion, in this war of words and conflicting theories. Our business is to answer back wisely, modestly, and yet grandly. (Excerpted from a speech by Frederick Douglass)[1]

One Hundred Years Later

Speaking at the 27th anniversary of the abolition of slavery in the District of Columbia, on April 16, 1889, Frederick Douglass defined with great clarity the central questions that were raised in that day, and 100 years later are being raised once again. In Douglass' words our business is to "answer back wisely, modestly, and yet grandly." The questions that are raised are neither isolated nor without merit. They are raised by ruling elites and by ordinary citizens. They are being raised by communities, by religious leaders, and by the parents of many of the young men who are the subject of this report. Most importantly, these are questions that are being raised by the minority group in which these young men are co-members. It so happens that these questions are framed today around the issue of a particular portion of African-American men and boys who are not a part of either the legitimate economic structure or the body politic of the country. Nor are they in community with their own ethnic group; rather, they pose a critical problem of interpersonal violence on the corridors and thoroughfares through which all Americans must pass. Consequently, the issues raised here have to do with how to assimilate, integrate, and restructure the lives of a particular group of individuals who, it would appear, have either lost their direction or lost hope, or both. All of these things combined pose a threat and disruption to the normal process of social life within communities and on the nation's streets.

What Douglass did in his speech was to outline his general sentiments regarding questions concerning the character of the African-American and his participation in normal American life as well as his ideas for the need of the African-American community of the late 19th century to determine its own character and fate apart from verbal and political attacks upon its being. The question in its broadest sense that Douglass sought to answer in the late 19th century and that must be answered now in the late 20th century is

> *How can a group be protected from public dissection as if it existed as a mere aberration in the society, and how to create for that group a concept that is able to sustain it as a self-respecting minority group within the majority society?*

This requires an assessment of the problems that are inherent within the particular group of young men who are at the heart of the issue and who, for a number of reasons not always of their own making, find themselves outside the mainstream, unable to regain entry into the general society. They see their living conditions, as well as the culture that they have created, used by others as the reasons for their own destruction and for the decline of American civilization.

Even though a segment of African-American men may be isolated from American society, they are crucial to its psyche. They are scapegoats, a political football, and the perfect multimedia ratings getter. This Task Force seeks to lay the groundwork for long-term sustained approaches to putting these issues to rest.

Background To The Task Force Report

Leadership grantmakers seek to bring about creative responses to the challenges facing society through a strengthened, enlightened, and broadened leadership. A critical issue facing the United States is the deepening crisis surrounding a segment of the African-American male population. A strengthened, enlightened, and broadened group of leaders should be able to design workable solutions that can deliver the appropriate economic and human services to this population. Consequently, a strategy that supports new community leadership, focusing on multiple interventions for these young men, boys, and their families, is crucial.

In March 1991, the W. K. Kellogg Foundation consulted with 34 individuals with first-hand knowledge of the issues facing certain African-American men and boys. The Foundation invited editors, ministers, scholars, and community leaders—specifically, community practitioners, those who are actively engaged in making a difference for young men in their respective communities. These practitioners are the people who have direct knowledge of and relationship to the problems. They are the people who can demonstrate some manner of success with their interventions. For this working consultation, the Foundation sought people who could help shape its response to the crisis through leadership grantmaking.

They made it clear that there would be no "quick fix," that time and money would have to be invested, and that the issues had to be raised at the national level so all Americans could be made aware of what was happening. They were just as emphatic in stating that there are persons who have been successful in changing the lives of young men in crisis, and that these persons should be recruited to begin a national dialogue, through which these destabilizing forces could be counteracted.

A national conference led by grassroots and community practitioners was held in Washington, D.C., in 1992. This event, sponsored jointly by the W. K. Kellogg Foundation and the National Urban Coalition, headed by Dr. Ramona Edelin, highlighted the need for a vision that would encompass all persons who work with these young men and their families.

From the discussions among community practitioners and the scholarly papers presented, there came advice and recommendations that led to the development of a vision statement and the establishment of the National Task Force on African-American Men and Boys. The emphasis throughout all these deliberations was on the centrality of viewing this issue in a holistic way and understanding that a national dialogue was necessary to reach solutions.

Vision Statement

We will support communities characterized by service and a keen sense of ethical behavior and moral responsibility. In these communities, we will continue to develop individuals and families who give voice to an innovative and entrepreneurial impulse. We will work to create communities grounded in cooperation, industry, self-reliance, and prosperity. We know this quest to be a cultural mission, as we re-examine and strengthen our ancient African sensibilities, and as we grow, develop, and inform our American experience. We envision this mission as one of reclamation—reclamation of the common good and our common culture, as well as reclamation of the neighborhoods and institutions which nurture our families. We understand that once this internal healing is begun, its effect will be the healing of a nation.

This statement crafted from the conference which recommended the creation of the National Task Force has guided the work of the Task Force and the preparation of this report.

The Task Force consists of forty-seven individuals. The Chairman is the former Ambassador to the United Nations and former Mayor of the City of Atlanta, Andrew J. Young, who now serves as co-chair of the Atlanta Olympic Committee. The Task Force Co-Chairs are the Reverend Calvin Butts of the Abyssinian Baptist Church in New York City, and Mr. Bertram Lee, the President/Director of Albimar Communications, Inc., in Washington, D.C. The Task Force Executive Director is Bobby Austin of the W.K. Kellogg Foundation in Battle Creek, MI.

The other members of the Task Force are as follows:

Ewart G. Abner, Executive Assistant to the Chairman, Gordy Company, Los Angeles, CA

Dennis Archer, Mayor, Detroit, MI

George Ayers, President, Ayers and Associates, Reston, VA

Lerone Bennett, Johnson Publishing Company, Chicago, IL

Chuck Blitz, Executive Director, Social Ventures Network, Santa Barbara, CA

Senator William Bowen, Grandin House, Cincinnati, OH

Peggy Cooper Cafritz, Founder/Vice President for Development, Duke Ellington School of the Arts, Washington, D.C.

Milton Davis, National President, Alpha Phi Alpha Fraternity, Tuskegee, AL

Tommy Dortch, ACMC-Atlanta, Inc., National 100 Black Men, Atlanta, GA,

David Driskell, Professor of Art, University of Maryland, College Park, MD

Gerald Freund, President, Private Funding Associates, New York, NY

Anthony Fugett, Director, TLC Beatrice International Holdings, Inc., New York, NY

Jeffrey Furman, Board of Directors, Ben and Jerry's Ice Cream, Ithaca, NY

C. E. Gibson, President, Federation of Masons of the World and

Eastern Stars, Detroit, MI

Tyrone Gilmore, Sr., Grand Basileus, Omega Psi Phi Fraternity, Inc., Spartanburg, SC

Joseph J. Givens, All Congregations Together, New Orleans, LA

John Goss, IBPO-Elks of the World, Knoxville, TN

Robert L. Harris, Grand Polemarch, Kappa Alpha Psi Fraternity, Inc., San Francisco, CA

Frances Hesselbein, President/CEO, Peter F. Drucker Foundation, New York, NY

Vernon Jarrett, Columnist, Chicago Sun Times, Chicago, IL

Timothy Jenkins, Publisher/CEO, Unlimited Visions, Inc., Washington, D.C.

Sharon Pratt Kelly, Mayor, Washington, D.C.

Debra Lee, President/CEO, Black Entertainment Television, Washington, D.C.

Reverend Michael Lemmons, Executive Director, Congress of National Black Churches, Washington, D.C.

Rick Little, President, International Youth Foundation, Battle Creek, MI

O. C. Lockett, President General, Grand Masonic Congress, USA, Detroit, MI

Haki Madhubuti, Founder/Publisher, Third World Press, Chicago, IL

Marilyn Melkonian, President, Telesis Corporation, Washington, D.C.

E. L. Palmer, Executive Director, Comprand, Inc., Chicago, IL

N. Joyce Payne, Director, Office for the Advancement of Public Black Colleges, Washington, D.C.

Wilbur Peer, Administrator, Rural Development Administration, Department of Agriculture, Washington, D.C.

Huel Perkins, President, Sigma Pi Phi Fraternity, Louisiana State University, Baton Rouge, LA

John Perkins, President, John Perkins Foundation, Pasadena, CA

Henry Ponder, President, Fisk University, Nashville, TN

Reverend Samuel D. Proctor, Rutgers University, New Brunswick, NJ

Kay George Roberts, Professor of Music, University of Massachusetts, Cambridge, MA

Michael Schultz, Producer/Director, Four Winds Film Corporation, Santa Monica, CA

Georgia Sorenson, Director, Center for Political Leadership, and Participation, University of Maryland, College Park, MD

Nelson Standifer, Director, Midnight Basketball Leagues, Inc., Hyattsville, MD

William Stanley, National President, Phi Beta Sigma, Atlanta, GA

Joe Stewart, Senior Corporate Vice President, Kellogg Company, Battle Creek, MI

Bernard Watson, Chairman, HMA Foundation, Inc., Philadelphia, PA

Robert L. Watson, President/CEO, Lauren, Watson and Co., Phoenix, AZ

Cordell Wynn, President, Stillman College, Tuscaloosa, AL

The National Task Force held its first meeting April 6, 1994, in Ypsilanti, Michigan. It completed its year-long deliberations by meeting in Washington, D.C.; at Fisk University, Nashville, Tennessee; and at The Martin Luther King Jr. Center for Non-Violent Social Change, Atlanta, Georgia. In this Report the Task Force is now prepared to share its findings, thoughts, and recommendations regarding the future of African-American men and boys in American society.

Dialogue with community leaders and citizens initiated this entire process. It is necessary, therefore, to go back to the African-American community to discuss with them our recommendations. As such, the Kellogg Foundation has joined with the Kettering Foundation to use their National Issues Forum to create an Internal Dialogue with African-American citizens reflecting on these issues. In this way, the Task Force will be able to do something that has rarely been done before: create a living document that includes many viewpoints and creates continued dialogue into the future, a dialogue that is supported by scholarship and practical experiences and contains recommendations that have been and can be widely discussed in community forums, university classrooms, and within the halls of government.

2 A PROFILE OF AFRICAN-AMERICAN MALES

MANY segments of the American population are raising questions about that portion of African-American men and boys for whom violence and street crime have become synonymous. These boys, themselves, and their families are also raising questions of their own regarding their relative position in American society.

Individuals who work with this troubled population continually refer to the fact that these young men are searching not only for a piece of the American dream, but they are attempting to define just how they came to be in this place and at this time. How to reconstruct and to reconnect are not unreasonable questions to ask. In fact, in their search for answers young African-American men and boys should view their youth as one of the most important times in their lives, and should see themselves as the heirs to a strong tradition of grassroots democracy, intellectual discourse, cultural development, and spiritual awakening. Instead, they find themselves at a point in their lives where it appears that life itself means very little.

Yet their quest, which when put beside all the questions that the society itself is raising about them, builds this issue into a mighty torrent of misconceptions, falsehoods, prejudices, misplaced aggressions, loves, and hates. If any of this is to be sorted out so that we can begin the steps needed, there must be a first step to reconnect these young men to themselves, to their families, to their communities, to their nation, and ultimately to the world.

It is not the intention of this report to answer all of these questions. However, it is incumbent upon those who seek to provide support, facilitation, and leadership in this society to respond to these young men and at least sketch an outline relative to these questions.

In the first section of this chapter we lay out in broad strokes the journey of this descendant of an African female who was perhaps the early mother of humankind to the American South and then to the American urban street corner.

In the remainder of the chapter, this young man's statistical profile in American society is discussed.

Who Am I And How Did I Get Here?

Picture a young man standing on any major street corner in America, possibly in a run-down, environmentally degraded, economically devastated, dilapidated area in any major urban or midsize American city. He has a baseball cap on backwards, a gold chain or two around his neck, gold wrist watch and rings, very baggy pants that sag, more than likely a sweater or jacket with a hood, the hood perhaps pulled over his head, and he may be wearing shade glasses. He might have a boom box that blares out rap music at its most vulgar, a seemingly debased scream, a primal scream at that, which announces to the world his and his peers' feelings of disgust, hatred, love, mixed and confused emotions. This young man may be in great trouble, may be standing on the corner preparing for trouble, or he may just be teetering on the brink of finding trouble.

Youth workers tell us that these young men are asking these questions: Who am I, and more importantly, how did I get here? Many scholars, social science practitioners, and particularly museum experts could help as we begin to outline an answer..

In the catalogue of an exhibition held at the Afro-American Historical and Cultural Museum of Philadelphia, in 1991, called "Let This Be Your Home—The African-American Migration to Philadelphia 1900–1940," the young man might learn this:

. . . Once that quest for connection is fixed in your mind, it becomes very difficult to dislodge as thousands of black genealogists and hundreds of black family reunions every year indicate. Certainly, anyone who tries to retrace that trail should know about the great migration of 1916–1923. That is the name of the movement from the South during and after World War I.

That was the basis for the changing of African-Americans from an overwhelming rural people to an overwhelmingly urban people, from a mainly southern people to a northern and southern people, and from farm workers to factory workers. Many African-American women became domestic workers. Up North came the southern folk coming from Mississippi to Detroit and Chicago; from Texas and Louisiana to California; from Tarboro, North Carolina to New York City; from Georgia to Trenton, and of course from all those places but especially from Maryland, Delaware, Virginia, South Carolina, North Carolina, and Georgia to Philadelphia, Pennsylvania.[2]

But, of course, that would only lead to the next question: How did I get to the Southern United States, to Mississippi, Alabama, and Georgia? Another museum exhibition called "Homecoming— African-American Family History in Georgia" outlines for these young men the how of that question.

In the late 1760s, however, ships directly from African ports began arriving in Georgia with groups of 100–300 slaves. These originated from the coast of West Africa, a pattern of origin much like South Carolina slave imports. In fact, in addition to direct trade with Africa, Georgia received many slaves from Charleston. It has been estimated that one of every four Africans brought to the North American mainland from 1619-1807 entered through Charleston. To the extent that Georgia slave imports reflect those reported for South Carolina, Black Georgians during the second half of the 18th century would have come primarily from the coast of present day Senegal, Gambia, Ivory Coast, Liberia, Guinea, and particularly in the later period of the slave trade, Central Africa commonly referred to then as Congo or Angola. There was apparently a bias in the Georgia and South Carolina markets against slaves from the Niger and cross river regions of present day Nigeria. The Ibo, for example, were reputed among South Carolina planters to be of independent and sensitive spirit prone to suicide. They were imported, however, in large numbers by other North American colonies and constitute an important people of origin for African-Americans.

The Africans who came to Georgia then were from very specific areas of the continent. Contrary to the conclusions of early scholars, they came primarily from that portion of Africa that lay within 300 miles of the west coast between the Senegal and Congo rivers.[3]

The pieces of the puzzle then begin to take shape so that the young man raising the questions can receive answers, not very pleasant answers, but answers nonetheless. They speak to the struggle and the travail of the African within the American context. Complicated questions, however, require more complicated responses. The most helpful way to see this issue of the African in the western world is probably to work at it through various frameworks, to view the image, the personhood, and the relationships between people on the African continent and those who came into contact with these people, people of dark skin as opposed to people of lighter skin. Then, of course, it might be important to say that at present many scholars and anthropologists seem to believe that the human race originated on the African continent. Many go so far as to say that all of mankind, the entire family tree, leads to an African female or a group of African females who constitute the early mothers of humankind. Appearing in the *Washington Post* on January 13, 1987, was an article entitled "All Family Tree Leads to Eve, a Scientist Concludes." What is discussed is the genetic analysis which indicates that there is a common ancestor some 200,000 years ago that connects all of mankind. The claim is not, of course, that "every person is descended from one Eve or that she was the only woman having children 200,000 years ago. She had many contemporaries who were each among the ancestors of many living today." This, of course, is not by itself a shocking assumption given the fact that the eastern coast of Africa from Ethiopia through Tanzania has been one of the most fertile areas for the discovery of ancient, prehistoric skeletons and fragments of both human and humanoid types which date back millions of years.

One of the most astounding was the finding of the very small four-foot, almost complete, skeleton of a human-like anthropoid in Ethiopia near the small, muddy Hagar river in a place called Hadar, several hundred miles from Addis Ababa. This partial skeleton, which is considered to be at least 3.5 million years old and was discovered in 1974 and named Lucy, is considered one of the major links between those of us who consider ourselves human beings today and our first erect-walking ancestors of eons ago. Furthermore, there are some, including many African tribes, who see themselves as the center of God's creation and believe that it was God himself who created man and placed him within the lush gardens of Africa.

The importance of western thought regarding the development and evolution of man is important, and these findings concerning this continent should be known to these young men on the street corners of America. They should know that Africa is a diverse continent, two times the land size of the United States with more than fifty-two countries and numerous ethnic and linguistic groups within the continent itself, that African beliefs are as varied and as many as there are tribes and nations upon that continent, but it is important to know that the African has since time immemorial had a strong belief in God. There are numerous facets from which religious and spiritual life are developed. It is important that the young man understand that Africans believe that God is spirit. "One of the most explicit descriptions of God as spirit occurs in a traditional pygmy hymn which says, . . .

In the beginning was God, Today is God, Tomorrow will be God. Who can make an image of God? He has no body. He is as a word which comes out of your mouth. That word it is no more. It has passed, and still it lives! So is God." [4]

This profound hymn should be the hymn that every African-American boy in every urban village in America utters, because at its most profound level, it states that which the Christian and Muslim faiths also state: that God is, was, and will forever be, and in the beginning was the word and that word was God. The connection between the spirit and soul of the Africans brought long ago to this continent from their spiritual home in Africa is a vibrant and real connection to God as spirit, God as word, and God as the unknowable and unexplainable.

These spiritual tenets become extremely important in the attempt to help men, boys, and their families re-create their past and focus on their future. It is ultimately "the substance of things hoped for and the evidence of things unseen."

African-American Males:
The Ongoing Struggle for Equality and Access

The African-American male holds a peculiar, uncertain status in American society. In some realms of life, such as athletics and entertainment, he is a highly respected, often revered figure. More generally, however, the African-American male is too often labeled as the epitome of all that is violent and criminal in our society. There is almost no awareness of African-American males who work as scientists, teachers, or in as wide a variety of jobs as white males. The larger society, however, does hold a range of perceptions concerning the character or nature of white males. It is an accepted fact that white males perform many different roles in society and that they are not, for example, either a Larry Bird or a Jeffrey Dahmer. Such an either/or perception is often applied to black males.

This kind of contradictory perception regarding African-American males is not new. There has been a long history of conflict between African-American males and the larger society. Today we see continuing aspects of this conflict when we look, for example, at the money being spent to build new prisons compared to the smaller amounts spent to promote educational opportunities for African-American males. Research shows that the basis of such conflicts and such contradictory policies and perceptions is firmly rooted in the history of American society and in the history of the African-American male's struggle to achieve his rightful place in that society.

The following section provides a statistical overview of the status of African-American men and boys, answering such questions as, who are they and where are they?

General Population

The total U.S. population is 248,709,873. The total African-American population is 29,930,524 (12%). Of this number, 14,170,151 are males.

The majority (52.8%) of African-Americans live in the South, 15,813,064. There are 5,606,793 blacks in the Northeast; 5,700,768 in the Midwest; and 2,809,899 in the West.[5]

The following table gives a broad picture of the distribution of African-Americans across the nation:

TABLE 1

STATES AND CITIES WITH THE LARGEST AFRICAN-AMERICAN POPULATIONS

State/City (with 100,000+ African-Americans)	Population
New York:	2,860,590
New York City	2,107,137
California:	2,198,766
Los Angeles	485,949
Oakland	163,526
San Diego	103,668
Texas:	2,018,543
Houston	457,574
Dallas	297,018
Florida:	1,755,958
Jacksonville	164,006
Georgia:	1,744,882
Atlanta	264,213
Illinois:	1,690,855
Chicago	1,086,389
North Carolina:	1,455,340
Charlotte	126,128
Louisiana:	1,298,662
New Orleans	308,364
Michigan:	1,289,012
Detroit	778,456
Maryland:	1,188,930
Baltimore	435,619
Virginia:	1,163,068
Richmond	112,406
Ohio:	1,152,230
Cleveland	235,053
Pennsylvania:	1,087,570
Philadelphia	632,430
South Carolina:	1,040,010
New Jersey:	1,035,386
Newark	161,084
Alabama:	1,019,743
Birmingham	168,464
Mississippi:	915,858
Jackson	109,587
Tennessee:	777,041
Memphis	334,981
Missouri:	546,850
St. Louis	187,995
Washington, D.C.	399,751

Health

African-American males face a number of serious health problems. This is in part reflected by the fact that between 1985 and 1991 the difference in life expectancy widened between black and white males. (See Tables 2 and 3.)

TABLE 2

LIFE EXPECTANCY AT BIRTH BY RACE AND SEX: U.S. 1970–1991

	1970	1975	1980	1985	1988	1989	1990	1991
White Male	68.0	69.5	70.7	71.8	72.2	72.5	72.7	72.9
Black Male	60.0	62.4	63.8	65.0	64.4	64.3	64.5	64.6

(Source: National Center for Health Statistics, 1994)

TABLE 3

HIV INFECTION MORTALITY
Death rates for HIV infection by race: U.S. 1987–1991

	1987	1988	1989	1990	1991
White Male	8.4	10.0	13.2	15.0	16.7
Black Male	25.4	31.6	40.3	44.2	52.9

(Source: National Center for Health Statistics, 1994)

Homicide

Homicide rates in 1991 for African-American males were 72.5 per 100,000, nearly 8 times higher than for white males. Homicide is the second leading cause of death among black children. It is the leading cause of death among black youth 15–24, and the second leading cause of death among black males ages 25–44.[6]

Family Life

Of the 7,055,063 black families, 3,045,283, or 43 percent, are headed by black females. 26.3 percent of all black families live in poverty, compared to 7.0 percent of white families. Of the 1,852,014 African-American families in poverty, 1,356,384, or 73 percent are headed by females. A key statistic in examining African-American family life is the qualitative difference in income between married couples with children under 18 and similarly situated female-headed households (see Table 4).

TABLE 4

MEDIAN INCOME OF AFRICAN-AMERICAN FAMILIES

	Median Income
Black married couples with children under 18	$35,162
Black female-headed households children under 18	9,534
White married couples with children under 18	41,686
White female-headed households with children under 18	15,011

(Source, U.S. Census, 1992)

This large income disparity points to both high rates of teenage pregnancy and to the increasingly lower rates of marriage among African-American males. In turn, marriage rates among black males are fundamentally influenced by their income levels. The higher the level of income, the more likely are African-American males to marry and establish stable, two-parent families. Thus family life must be seen as a central component in fostering the well-being of the African-American community.[7]

Education

Table 5 shows the current status for African-American males in education:

TABLE 5

EDUCATIONAL ATTAINMENT OF AFRICAN-AMERICAN MALES 15 YEARS AND OVER

High School	2,762,541
Associates Degree	
Occupational	214,863
Academic	192,752
Bachelor	586,014
Master	191,068
Professional	58,109
Doctorate	32,335

In the central cities, African-American students make up 32.5 percent of the total student population.

Of the 1,751,414 African-Americans enrolled in college, 40.9 percent are African-American males.[8] As shown in Table 6, the rate of bachelor's degrees earned by African-American males in 1991 did not equal the number of B.A.s earned in 1977.

TABLE 6

NUMBER OF DEGREES EARNED BY AFRICAN-AMERICAN MALES: 1977–1991

1977	1979	1981	1985	1987	1989	1990	1991
25,147	24,659	24,511	23,018	22,499	22,363	23,264	24,326

(Source: National Center for Educational Statistics)

A far worse pattern exists for master's and doctoral degrees. In 1977 African-American males earned 7,781 master's degrees. In 1991, they earned only 5,707. African-American males earned 766 Ph.D.s in 1977, but earned only 582 Ph.D.s in 1991. This number represents only little more than an average of 11 Ph.D.s per state for African-American males, and points out the chronic problem of African-American underrepresentation in graduate schools across the nation.[9]

The various numbers for both bachelor's, master's, and doctoral degrees strongly indicate the positive effects for African-American males of the affirmative educational practices and policies that were pursued in the late 1960s and early 1970s. Now, however, universities across the country have already or are in the process of eliminating these affirmative, results-producing programs, which will most likely have an even greater negative effect on African-American male degree completion rates.

As Green states, "Although white Americans often find it difficult to comprehend the extent of discrimination in this country, the facts show that American society has routinely and systemically limited the opportunities for minorities. This discrimination has been particularly apparent in the public schools."[10] With more policies being implemented throughout the educational spectrum, from proficiency testing in high schools to eliminating support programs for minorities at universities, there is every reason to fear that the educational opportunities for African-American males and other minorities could well become even more limited.

Incarceration

For the first time in history the United States prison population has exceeded one million. There are 1,115,111 prisoners in state and federal prison, 508,084 are African-American, 469,751 are African-American males.[11]

Figures from the Bureau of Justice show the following breakdown for state prisons:

TABLE 7

ESTIMATED NUMBER OF AFRICAN-AMERICAN MALES IN STATE PRISONS, 1991

Age	18–19	20–24	25–29	30–34	35–39	40 and older
Number Incarcerated	13,600	62,500	82,600	72,000	46,000	47,800

(Source: Bureau of Justice Bulletin, 1994)

The United States has the highest incarceration rates in the world. More people are imprisoned than in Russia or in the former police state of South Africa. This higher incarceration rate has the most negative and profound effect on African-American males.[12]

Yet it is important to keep in mind that the large majority of African-American males are not out breaking the law but are instead engaged in the everyday activities of trying to make a way for themselves and their families. In this regard, it should be pointed out that the number of black males (16 years or older) who are incarcerated represents 4.8 percent of all black males in these age groups. This percentage is disproportional and unacceptably high since black men constitute more than 50 percent of the male prison population. At the same time, however, this percentage also reflects the fact that well over 95 percent of black males (16 years and older) are not in prison.

Poverty

The rate of poverty for all African-Americans is 29.5 percent, compared to a 9.8 percent poverty rate for whites. Rates of poverty for African-American males are shown in Table 8.

TABLE 8

POVERTY RATES FOR AFRICAN-AMERICAN MALES

Age	Total	Number Poor	% Poor
TOTAL	14,731,000	4,197,000	29%
Under 18 Years	5,275,000	2,382,000	45%
18–24	1,654,000	395,000	24%
25–34	2,505,000	432,000	17%
35–44	2,027,000	340,000	17%
45–54	1,235,000	195,000	16%
55–59	538,000	87,000	16%
60–69	439,000	95,000	22%
65-older	1,058,000	271,000	26%

(Source: U.S Census, 1992)

Employment

TABLE 9

LABOR FORCE PARTICIPATION RATES FOR AFRICAN-AMERICAN MALES

Age	Total	Employed	Unemployed	% Unemployed
16 & Over	6,911,000	5,957,000	954,000	14%
16–19	413,000	247,000	166,000	40%
20–24	854,000	658,000	196,000	23%
25–34	2,115,000	1,854,000	261,000	12%
35–44	1,788,000	1,600,000	188,000	11%
45–54	1,050,000	964,000	85,000	8%
55–64	566,000	515,000	51,000	9%
65 & Over	126,000	119,000	7,000	4%

TABLE 10

UNEMPLOYMENT RATES BY RACE AND GENDER: 1972–1994
(population 16 years and over)

Year	Race/Gender			
	White		Black	
	Males	Females	Males	Females
1972	4.5	5.9	9.3	11.8
1973	3.8	5.3	8.0	11.1
1974	4.4	6.1	9.8	11.3
1975	7.2	8.6	14.8	14.8
1976	6.4	7.9	13.7	14.9
1977	5.5	7.3	13.3	14.9
1978	4.6	6.2	11.8	13.8
1979	4.5	5.9	11.4	13.3
1980	6.1	6.5	14.5	14.0
1981	6.5	6.9	5.7	15.6
1982	8.8	8.3	20.1	17.6
1983	8.8	7.9	20.3	18.6
1984	6.4	6.5	16.4	15.4
1985	6.1	6.4	15.3	14.9
1986	6.0	6.1	14.8	14.2
1987	5.4	5.2	2.7	13.2
1988	4.7	4.7	11.7	11.7
1989	4.5	4.0	11.4	9.8

Year	Race/Gender			
	White		Black	
	Males	**Females**	**Males**	**Females**
1990	4.7	4.1	11.3	9.8
1991	6.6	5.5	12.8	12.0
1992	6.5	5.5	14.4	12.9
1993	5.7	4.9	11.3	10.6
1994	4.7	4.1	9.1	9.1

(Source: Handbook of Labor Statistics, 1989;
Employment and Earnings, January 1990.

Note: comparable employment figures for blacks and whites are available
only from 1972 on)

The pattern of unemployment for both black males and black females, contrasted with that of their white counterparts, is disheartening. In the period 1990–1994 the black male unemployment rate is more than twice that of white males. Although discrimination is a likely factor, educational attainment is also a significant factor. The high drop-out rates of African-Americans in urban areas is not viewed favorably by employers. School completion is essential to job acquisition. Encouraging African-Americans to attain a complete education at the highest levels possible must be a national priority.

The unemployment figures are, in general, very high, but the percentages for young African-American males 16–24 are alarmingly high. The high rates of unemployment for these age categories are even more disturbing considering that these are typically the years when young men are in the process of choosing careers and making related fundamental decisions about their futures. These chronic high unemployment rates explain much of the sense of dislocation and despair that exists among African-American males and within the African-American community in general. As Green notes, "The effects of unemployment extend beyond the immediate consequences of economic instability and financial hardships. Indeed, the condition of being unemployed generates diverse family and social problems."[13]

Despite the high poverty rates, for example, of African-Americans, 29.5 percent compared to 9.8 percent for whites, this number also means that the majority of African-Americans, 70.5 percent, do not live in poverty. Yet from the discussions in Congress and elsewhere about welfare reform, one might be led to believe that these poverty figures were just the opposite.

Whereas it is true that poverty and unemployment are dispro-portionately high among African-American males, it is also impor-tant to note some of the positive achievements black males are mak-ing in economic terms. For instance, of the 6,911,000 black males (16 and older) in the labor force, 782,210 of that number, (11.3 per-cent) are in managerial and professional positions. While it is a fact that black males typically do not have earnings equal to their white counterparts, nevertheless, black males with a B.A. or better do have respectable median incomes, as noted in Table 11.

TABLE 11

INCOME OF COLLEGE-EDUCATED AFRICAN-AMERICAN MALES

Degree Level for Black Men	B.A.	M.A.	Ph.D.	Professional
Median Earnings	$33,656	40,743	52,276	63,998

These income levels are reflective of the hundreds of thousands of African-American males who are forming stable, two-parent fami-lies and are playing a major role in nurturing African-American young men and boys to become responsible and productive members of their communities.

Perhaps the figures that most symbolize the will and determi-nation of African-American males to succeed are those for B.A.s earned between 1977 and 1991. These figures, referred to in the body of the report, are listed in Table 12 for easy reference.

TABLE 12

NUMBER OF DEGREES EARNED BY AFRICAN-AMERICAN MALES: 1977–1991

1977	1979	1981	1985	1987	1989	1990	1991
25,147	24,659	24,511	23,018	22,499	22,363	23,264	24,326

(Source: National Center for Educational Statistics)

The totals show that 1977 was the high point, with black males that year earning 25,147 B.A.s. The numbers steadily dropped after that. This continuous decline was a reflection of the systematic reduction in the affirmative policies that had done so much to promote expanded educational opportunities for black males (and females). Nevertheless, despite the cutbacks in scholarships, loans, and despite the elimination of more flexible admissions policies, African-American males in 1991 still managed to earn nearly as many B.A.s as in the high-point year.

This notable achievement is undoubtedly a result of the increased efforts in mentoring on the part of older black males, of black families sacrificing to support the education aspirations of their children, and of black individuals and institutions contributing even more to foster the education of young black men and boys. Such success shows what can be accomplished when African-American males and their community work in concert for positive ends. This is also the kind of success that needs to be made more visible both within and outside the African-American community. The sizable core of upright, hard-working, accomplished African-American men must no longer be overlooked and invisible. Making their efforts and their example more widely known will provide young African-American men and boys with a firm basis on which to build their futures.

Conclusion

African-American males (and the larger African-American community) have faced continuous forms of mistreatment and oppression. The denial of the opportunity to vote, the denial of higher-paying industrial jobs, the denial of educational opportunities, and other related forms of racial discrimination all reflected practices and policies deeply rooted in American thought and American traditions. And the consequences of these historical practices are still very much with us today. When we see, for example, African-American males with disproportionately higher imprisonment rates, disproportionately higher unemployment rates, disproportionately higher poverty rates, but disproportionately lower educational attainment rates, it is clear that these facts represent a continuation of the long history of racial discrimination in the country.

High unemployment, high rates of imprisonment and poverty—these are the difficult social and institutional barriers that African-American males must daily try to overcome in the effort to establish a place for themselves in society. It is little wonder that many

African-American males give up in hopelessness. Nor is it any wonder, as African-American males feel themselves abandoned by much of the rest of society, that they give in to the growing rage they feel. The tragic consequences of this rage are everywhere around us, both within and outside the African-American community. Among these tragic consequences are the losses to all society of the contributions from the great number of African-American males who fall victim to the obstacles that surround them. Although this Report addresses the plight of African-American men, it is understood that the plight of African-American females is inextricably related and tied to that of African-American males.

Nevertheless, it is crucial to note that despite the many obstacles, today, as in the past, there are significant numbers of African-American males who succeed at all levels of American society. Richard Parsons, for example, has recently been named president of the media giant Time-Warner. Dr. Benjamin Carson is a world authority on brain surgery and was the first neurosurgeon to successfully separate Siamese twins joined at the head. Delano Lewis is president and chief executive of National Public Radio. Douglas Wilder in 1990 was the first African-American ever elected governor. Colin Powell is the first African-American ever to head the post of Chairman of the Joint Chiefs of Staff, and has been widely considered as a presidential or vice-presidential candidate. More broadly, nearly all sectors of American society are affected by Garrett Morgan's invention of the traffic light. And just as significantly has American society been affected by Charles Drew's scientific advances in the preservation of blood.

Such a listing of prominent African-Americans could be extended indefinitely. At the same time it is just as important to note the many other instances of less well-known African-American males who are achieving success.

For instance, on the secondary-school level, the Piney Woods School in Mississippi, under the leadership of Dr. Charles Beady, has an outstanding record of educating and graduating young black students. Over 75 percent of the students at this school are from poor, female-headed households, yet over 95 percent of the school's graduates go on to some of the best colleges and universities in the country. This year's graduating class of forty-eight students includes twenty-one African-American males. The average ACT score is 18.3. Each of the males has been accepted into college. Winners of this year's boys' state basketball championship, the Piney Woods team started four seniors. One of the seniors scored 17 on the ACT, and the other three scored 18 or above.

The Piney Woods example is extremely important. We are all well aware of the low academic scores and the high failure rates for African-American males in most urban schools. The accomplishments at Piney Woods show, however, that young African-American males (and females) can perform at the highest levels academically when provided with a nurturing, positive learning climate. Piney Woods' achievements confirm Green's (1969) conclusion that "students from disadvantaged urban (and rural) backgrounds can experience academic success when we arrange the environment in a manner that is appropriate to their needs."

At the collegiate level, the GEM program (National Consortium for Graduate Degrees for Minorities in Engineering and Science, Inc.) has assisted scores of African-American males in earning Ph.D.s in science and masters and Ph.D.s in engineering. For example, in the 1995 school year 65 of the 122 male Master's GEM Fellows are African-American males. Of the 12 male GEM Ph.D. Science Fellow Awards, nine are African-American. Of the ten male GEM Ph.D. Engineering Fellow Awards, eight are African-American.

Similarly, the Florida Endowment Fund, under the leadership of Dr. Israel Tribble, has significantly contributed to African-American males obtaining doctoral degrees at various universities in that state's higher education system. In fact, since its inception in 1984, the Florida Endowment Fund has assisted some 30 African-American males in completing their Ph.D. degrees in both social and physical sciences, including higher mathematics, chemistry, and engineering.

These few but illustrative examples speak to the great diversity of talents and skills that African-American males possess. From factory workers to physicists, from service workers to social scientists, from grassroots community activists to nationally recognized leaders, the broad range of activities and vocations African-American males are involved in is too often overlooked, particularly by the dominant media. All of these talents and skills, nonetheless, must be put to more effective use, for it is clear that African-American males must in large measure be the architects of their own betterment. Clearly in today's society, with many calling for less social and governmental assistance, African-American males themselves must take the lead in developing viable, nurturing, social, cultural, and economic institutions. This is a profound and, at times, seemingly overwhelming responsibility. As the foregoing brief history has shown, however, African-American males have continuously found the will, the resources, and the spirit not only to persevere, but to overcome.

3 EMERGING THEMES AND MAJOR RECOMMENDATIONS

*A*T a very fundamental level, the men and women who developed this report understood that leadership, dialogue, and systemic change are the three tools that must be used to rebuild the civic lives not only of this group of young men who are in trouble, but also of the nation.

Leadership and a Framework for Dialogue

When one puts the words of Frederick Douglass alongside Walter Lippman's insight into the public mind,[14] it is obvious that coming to grips with situations which involve complicated images, distortions, and prejudice is very difficult, and requires skillful handling.

Today, effective leadership continues to be seen as the necessary ingredient for helping the American public deal with one of its most complicated issues. In the context of the position of African-American men and boys in society, leadership is a key ingredient in pointing public opinion toward the change that must be made in understanding the human condition and the social realities that surround and underlie the basic problems associated with being both a minority and a racially different group within the United States.

To better understand the human condition and this social reality, a format must be created that will allow discussions to take place within the minority group itself, and between African-Americans and the national community.

James MacGregor Burns states, in his Pulitzer Prize-winning book *Leadership*:

Leadership is a process of morality to the degree that leaders engage with followers on the basis of shared motives and values and goals—on the basis, that is, of the followers' "true" needs as well as those of leaders . . . but only the followers themselves can ultimately define their own true needs. And they can do so only when they have been exposed to the competing diagnoses, claims, and values of would-be leaders, only when the followers can make an informed choice among competing "prescriptions," only when—in the political arena at least—followers have had full opportunity to perceive, comprehend, evaluate, and finally experience alternatives offered by those professing to be their "true" representatives. Ultimately the moral legitimacy of transformational leadership, and to a lesser degree transactional leadership, is grounded in conscious choice among real alternatives. Hence leadership assumes competition and conflict, and brute power denies it.[15]

The general discussion about crime and violence in the United States has been very much a canvas on which a portrait of a deeply troubled African-American boy and his community is painted by various politicians and the American media. In fact, this is not an untrue statement; statistics show that in proportion to their numbers in society, African-American boys play a major role in perpetuating crime and violence. When one piles up the death statistics, more young black men die from murder than from any other kind of health-related or accident-related occurrences.

What leadership has to do is not to explain away this particular phenomenon, but to help people to understand it: what it is about, what it says, what it does not say; and also, to make it clear that these boys are not the only purveyors of crime in this society. In fact, when general figures are used to describe issues of crime and punishment, it is obvious that African-American boys are not alone, by any stretch of the imagination, in the perpetuation of crime, either on the streets or in corporate America. Yet they have become the absolute symbol for such behavior.

The question is then far beyond just African-American men and boys, and yet it is directly related to these young men and their participation, and development either positively or negatively, within the body politic of the nation. Always mindful of these broad concerns, the National Task Force on African-American Men and Boys sought answers to the questions:

First: How to bring relief and assistance to communities and families that are experiencing the great hurt and harm of violent behavior.

Second: How to find a way to bring to light, through its recommendations, means to reestablish community and, thus, make inroads into violent behavior, the major social problem of the day.

Third: How to engage this large number of young men in constructive participation within American society while at the same time refurbishing the image that now has been unfairly placed upon the entire population of African-American men and boys, who suffer as a result of media and political short-sightedness and stereotyping.

The Task Force understands leadership to be a learned art; a behavior that, when learned, helps to create a new sense of reality, a new sense of purpose, and an engagement of dialogue with family, community, and society. It is in this context that the W. K. Kellogg Foundation decided to undertake its work with African-American men and boys.

The Reestablishment of Civil Society and Civic Life

DUTIES

And while we are demanding and ought to demand, and will continue to demand the rights . . . God forbid that we should ever forget to urge corresponding duties upon our people:

The duty to vote.

The duty to respect the rights of others.

The duty to work.

The duty to obey the laws.

The duty to be clean and orderly.

The duty to send our children to school.

The duty to respect ourselves even as we respect others.

This statement, complaint and prayer do we submit to the American people and Almighty God, 1905.

(Excerpted from *The Declaration of Principles of the Niagara Movement*, W. E. B. Du Bois.)[16]

The National Task Force on African-American Men and Boys was established to develop a comprehensive strategy for programs that could bring long-term sustaining interventions into the lives of young men and boys who are in trouble in American society. Many would have assumed that this Task Force and its work would have taken shape around the issue of violence. However, that was not the case. Because violence has been painted with a very broad brush in this society in which African-American men and boys are seen as the face of that violence, it was a momentous decision by both the Foundation and the Task Force to pull back from such simplistic approaches and stereotypes in their work to assist young men.

From the outset, the Task Force understood that violence is a symptom of a much larger problem, and that trying to cure violence by itself would not cure anything. It would, in fact, simply mean the building of more and more jails, the arming of more and more citizens, and perhaps even the possibility of a war against our own youth. This was unacceptable.

The Task Force report used the work of Peter Senge, author of *The Fifth Discipline*, to understand how to approach this pervasive situation. According to Senge, one must shift from "seeing the parts to the seeing of the whole." This allows a systems-wide approach to change—or systemic change—to be put into effect. This became the guiding principle for the work undertaken by the Task Force. There must be a dialogue on issues so that we can sift through and determine at what point to enter the system to make changes holistically for young boys and their families. This is necessary to stop the "Band-Aid" approach that seems to be in vogue in the majority of social policy planning and political arenas in the United States at present. The tool of systemic change allows for thinking on a much deeper level about why this disruption has occurred and why the disruption is symbolized by violence.

The Challenge to See the Whole System

A March 2, 1993, article appearing in the *Science Times* section of the *New York Times* discussed Interior Secretary Bruce Babbitt's announcement that the Interior Department would try to "prevent endangered species crisis by promoting the long term health care of whole ecological systems." This particular approach, new to government, is also somewhat new as far as public policy is concerned. It provides a new way of thinking about human beings and their environment. They are in symbiotic relationship, and it does little good to attempt to assist individuals in part without dealing with the whole.

When one assumes this position of the whole as opposed to its parts, it creates within the public mind a particular kind of relationship. Frederick Douglass describes this as consciousness.

Consciousness is to the soul and to society what the law of gravity is to the universe. It holds society together. It is the basis of all trust and confidence. It is the pillar of all moral rectitude. Without it, suspicion would take the place of trust, vice would be more than a match for virtue, men would prey upon other men like the wild beast of the desert, and earth would become hell.[17]

Consciousness supports new leadership learning which concentrates on seeing the whole as opposed to its parts, asserts a viewpoint that makes the critical leap toward understanding why the issue of African-American men and boys is of such importance, and what understanding could mean, not just for the African-American population, but also for the country in general. It expresses very clearly this concept: Once we have been able to bring character and self-reliance back to these boys, this would not only heal the wounds of this group of young men who are in trouble, but would contribute to the healing of the nation.

Consequently, if one is to find a cure, that cure will not only create wholeness for the individual, but wholeness for society as well.

The bottom line for the Task Force was to be able to bring healing to communities. That healing would begin the healing of the breached social, political, and economic systems of the nation.

As the Task Force moved through its work, it became obvious that all of its work, if it was to be systemic, would somehow have to be captured within a larger context. That context was the *human condition*.

The human condition, as defined by Dr. Joyce Payne, the Director of the Office of Public Black Colleges, took into account the fact that it is within a particular system that all individuals develop. Within the system in which African-American men and boys find themselves, there is a continual tearing away of opportunities, status, and self-respect. There is a degrading of the environment in which they live in inner cities and destructive lifestyles that make life extremely unhealthy, therefore creating mounting health problems. There is also the obvious deterioration of families disrupted by the lack of jobs, the lack of opportunity, and the complete gutting of the public education system.

Dr. Payne was joined later on in this Task Force discussion by Dr. Samuel D. Proctor, dean of African-American ministers and advisor to presidents Lyndon B. Johnson and John F. Kennedy, and the former deputy director of the Peace Corps, who brought to us the classic concept of the *polis*. He used this term in reference to life in the city. Proctor states that one has to have the ethics and etiquette to create the values that allows one to live as a citizen within the context of metropolitan life. These ideas, added together with words of wisdom from Ambassador Andrew Young concerning the politics of breached relationships in America's urban inner cities, established the idea of the human condition. From this the Task Force constructed a framework from which to understand why we are seeing such disruptions within these communities.

Having constructed this context, we were able to create the other themes which came out of the work of the Task Force itself—from *Polis*, to the development of *Civic Storytelling*, to the *Common Good*, to *Grassroots Civic Leadership*, to the *Restoration of Community Institutions*, and then finally to the establishment of a process for a national *Civic Dialogue* on these issues.

The United Nations has since 1990 issued a yearly *Human Development Report*. In the most recent report is a human development index that takes into consideration many of these same issues. (See appendix VII.) It became obvious that we could merge these two ideas, the idea of the *human condition* as articulated by the Task Force and the idea of *human development* as developed by the United Nations.

The following synopsis of the human development index gives a comprehensive framework within which to begin discussions on issues involving African-American men and boys. The concept of human development is a process of enlarging people's choices. It is based on universally accepted principles and rights of equal opportunity, access, and protection. It recognizes that all people should be able "to lead a long and healthy life, to acquire knowledge and to have access to the resources needed for a decent standard of living." But human development also recognizes that many people also want to pursue other choices, whether political, economic, social, or creative.

Human development thus has two sides. One is the formation of human capabilities—such as improved health, knowledge and skills. The other is the use people make of their acquired capabilities—for productive purposes, for leisure or for being active in cultural, social and political affairs. If the scales of human development do not finely balance the two sides, much human frustration can result.[18]

Major Recommendations

Overall, the Task Force has made sixty-one recommendations. These specific recommendations follow each theme chapter; however, three general recommendations were also made. These are general or overall recommendations that should be seen as separate and distinct from the specific recommendations. They form the foundation for the remainder of the recommendations. They comprise the first five-year plan, called *Project 2000*. Both Project 2000 and the action plan called the *Generation Plan* can be found at the end of Chapter 11.

First that a national work group be established to continue the work of the Task Force over the next decade. This work group would facilitate a dialogue among African-American civic, social, religious, and professional organizations to bring about the necessary changes that would support grassroots community leaders in urban America. The group would work collaboratively with grassroots leaders and communities to create strategic action plans that would facilitate new knowledge, information, resources, and revenue to help these communities as they develop their own activities to bring about change.

Second the Task Force recommends that a philanthropic organization be established that would support all of the major recommendations that have been made by this Task Force. The Task Force recommendations are numerous, they are broad, and they are varied. The only way that these ideas will be implemented is if funding can be found to sustain them over a long-term period. Assistance and facilitation will be needed to support the dynamism of grassroots democracy, already budding in these communities. Consequently, this funding agency would be created to disburse funds, to operate programs, and to act as a general philanthropic organ dedicated to the improvement of the conditions of African-American men and boys in particular. This organization could find additional support from civic, social, religious, and professional organizations. One idea would have each fraternity and sorority, civic or social organization in the country forgo one year of its national meetings and put whatever money would have supported that year's events into the philanthropic organization. These and other funds would provide leverage to build the organization.

Third a National Conversation on Race Relations must be facilitated. The boys' fate and that of the nation rests in our renewed ability to talk to one another. This facilitated national conversation would last through several decades. The Race Relations Institute at Fisk University should be supported. The Race Relations Institute would sustain and undergird a national conversation among all American citizens regarding the human condition as it exists in the United States and a discussion of the relationship between citizens and groups in furthering the democratic process in America. The Center for Living Democracy could collaborate on this project.

Themes

The National Task Force report and its recommendations are developed around the following themes:

Polis This is a comprehensive idea regarding the values, manners, morals, and etiquette that are needed for structuring public life in communities on both a social and political level. This idea of polis also defines community through the work of African-American intellectuals, thinkers, and politicians such as Fredrick Douglass, W. E. B. DuBois, Booker T. Washington, Martin Luther King, Jr., Charles S. Johnson, Patricia Roberts Harris, Howard Thurman, and Samuel D. Proctor.

Civic Storytelling Recommendations here focus around the issue of how these boys and their ancestors fit into American culture. Civic storytelling honors the life of the ordinary hero who successfully creates public kinship. Links are established through the arts, the humanities, and education. The civic story is told and retold, thus establishing one's place in society and creating public kinship.

Grassroots Civic Leadership Empowering individuals (parents, teachers, ministers, young people) to take control of their lives and communities is the key factor in this section. Programs to reinvent civil and economic life are developed. Proposals such as individual learning plans as a way to develop personal mastery and create individual personal capacity are noted.

Common Good How can we create common good? The focus is on the classical approach to the Wealth of Nations. How does the community create and meet common needs? The recommendations speak of entrepreneurship and economic development, educational reform, and many other exciting commonwealth ideas.

Restoring Community Institutions Here we discuss the elements for restructuring and reinventing civil and social life in communities. The collective will to forge new communities is sounded and includes issues concerning housing and the development of new funding organizations. Organizing devices, such as a calendar for purposes of structure, history, and worship, and the development of new apparatus for delivering grassroots multi-focused, multi-purpose programming to boys in these communities are presented.

Civic Dialogue Here the recommendations ask and answer: What are we talking about when we talk about African-American men and boys and their families? The issue in this section is to stress the fact that capacity is built through dialogue as opposed to hate and mistrust.

Glossary of Terms

This *glossary of terms* is provided to assist the reader in understanding the use of certain terms and phrases that occur in the Report.

Integrating the margins Defined by Olivier DéGeorges as the process of bringing the underclass, the out-groups, into the mainstream to improve their human development. It is the gathering of individuals into the social center (the Polis).

Polis Defined by Dr. Samuel D. Proctor as the establishment and teaching of particular values, manners, morals, and etiquette that are needed for structuring public life in communities. As a member of the polis (city-community) one must meet requirements. Entry into the polis carries with it a tacit "social contract." That tacit social contract implies that there are limits on the behavior of members of the polis.

Common good Dr. Frances Moore Lappé defines common good as a process where people agree in advance to seek the good through genuine dialogue. Its premise lies in the widely-shared values of a diverse people, values that form the basis of a renewed patriotism as love of country; pride in society; fairness with opportunity for all; pride in commitment to promote life; pride in seeing that no one is denied the essentials necessary to be a full member of society; and pride in safeguarding natural resources. We also use common good to mean economic development which engages communities to create shared economic opportunities.

Civic storytelling Civic storytelling is the recounting of those stories that lift the image, and show the ordinary citizen as a good, contributing part of society. This recounting reinforces the public relatedness of the individual to the whole of the community, and reinforces one's position in the society. This action is performed through the arts, humanities, and politics.

Urban insecurity The term "urban insecurity" describes the world-wide phenomena of intense change such as population destabilization, the international drug trade, aggressive world wide spread of organized crime activities, and a global high-tech economy, which have dramatically altered the environment in urban settings. Coupled with these profound changes in the public domain is the rapid growth of the underclass in the world's cities. These forces have created an entire population living outside of the society. Associated with this underclass are crime, violence, and major health issues.

Media mythology According to Dr. George Gerbner, media mythology is the fact that for the first time in our history, most of the stories told to most of the children most of the time are no longer told by parents. They are not hand crafted in the community, no longer by the school, no longer by the church, and very often no longer by anybody who really has anything to tell, but increasingly by a highly centralized, globalized group of conglomerates that have something to sell.

Public kinship Defined by Dr. Bobby Austin as the willingness to publicly assume responsibility in acting out the phrase "love thy neighbor as thyself." It is the public acknowledgment that we are family in our community, nations, and world, and that we act accordingly. It requires our leaders to establish foundations that support participation in the nation's public arena as well as promote community ethics.

Group position Dr. Herbert Blumer defines group position as a set of feelings which members of one racial group have toward the members of another racial group. Group position is not a mere summation of the feelings of position such as might be developed independently by separate individuals as they come to compare themselves with given individuals of the other race. Group position refers to the position of group to group, not to that of individual to individual.

Parallel economy Defined by Dr. Bobby Austin and Michael Shuman, as the development of a small-scale economy. It is a small-scale economic system rooted in the community.

Human development Defined by the United Nations Development Program as, first, the formation of human capabilities—such as improved health, knowledge, and skills. The use people make of their acquired capabilities for production purposes, for leisure, or for being active in cultural, social, and political affairs is the result of the capabilities.

Human condition Dr. Joyce Payne uses the term "human condition" to describe the quality of life of a community and its members. It includes elements that contribute to the well-being of the individual, such as safety, justice, income, education, and opportunity, among other things.

Systemic change According to Dr. Peter Senge a complete systemwide change is necessary. The issues in society must be approached as a whole system, as opposed to dealing with parts (issue by issue). This requires the breaking of certain patterns of behavior and thought to reorient our mental models so that they become models of reality that work. In Senge's work, mental models are built around ourselves, other people, and the outside world. Systemic change requires personal mastery and shared vision. Systems thinking and its change process is "how our actions influence our reality."

4 POLIS: A Renewed Concept of Community

*P*OLIS is a comprehensive idea that calls for the establishment and teaching of the particular values, manners, morals, and etiquette that are needed for structuring public life in communities. This idea was brought to the Task Force by Dr. Samuel D. Proctor, the former deputy director of the Peace Corps, Pastor of Abyssinian Baptist Church, theologian and scholar at Rutgers University, and author of the book, *The Substance of Things Hoped For*. This idea of polis also includes the work of many African-American intellectuals who have written on the issue of community such as Frederick Douglass, W. E. B. DuBois, Booker T. Washington, Martin Luther King, Jr., and Charles S. Johnson, among others.

Background

At the fourth meeting of the Task Force, Dr. Samuel D. Proctor delivered an address on the topic: "The Context for Communities and Youth Development: Community or Chaos?"[19]

He started from the premise that the resolution of the issues facing African-American men and boys in late twentieth-century America will require, first, the development and implementation of a set of new ideas, which must be both immediate and long-range in nature.

Proctor noted that "in a crisis like this, there are some emergency measures [that must take place] to ease the pain and to redirect the energies *immediately*."

Similarly, long-range vision is an essential component of any solution, because, according to Proctor, this kind of vision will allow

47

us "to be patient and courageous enough to live with those [immediate] ideas until they become *clearly* manifest."

Throughout this process of formulating a new set of ideas, however, we must be ever mindful of a fact Proctor regards as a fundamental: "We have a generation [of African-American youth] that is detached from the value system that nurtured those of us who are in this room."

Solutions, Proctor suggests, require reconciliation of the needs of three distinct, though not mutually exclusive, constituencies. First, we must try to reconcile the differences between the needs of our youth; and, second, the needs of our nation; and third, the needs of "the highest human values that we know."

The Idea of Polis

Drawing upon his enormous storehouse of personal knowledge and experience, Proctor reached back to his years of study as an undergraduate at Virginia Union University, where he and Simeon Booker, Washington Bureau Chief for Johnson Publishing Company's *Jet* magazine, were the last two students in Dr. Joshua B. Simpson's Greek class. It was here that he kept running across the word *polis*, which was simply translated as "city-state," with physical boundaries. Yet, he related, Simpson "made it clear that the word *polis* meant more than simply a geographic boundary. There was something else involved."

This something else was that the word *polis* carried with it at least two additional concepts. First, according to Proctor, if one was not a member of a polis; that is, if one lived outside of the polis, one could behave any way one wanted. There were no restrictions or limits on the behavior of those persons not living inside the polis.

On the other hand, once an individual crossed the boundary into a polis, that person's behavior had to change. Entry into the polis carried with it a tacit "social contract." This tacit social contract implied that there were limits on the behavior of members of the polis.

From this comes the notion that society has certain requirements and certain expectations regarding an individual's actions and the accompanying consequences. Moreover, these requirements and expectations are based upon a certain set of values that have been tacitly agreed upon by the members of the polis.

Today's young African-American males, Proctor asserts, possess an understanding of neither the existence of the polis nor its fundamental values. He implies that this set of circumstances has not always been a dominant feature of African-American youth culture, when he states "there is another class of African-Americans like ourselves, who were nurtured, taught how to live in the polis, benefited from it, with beautiful families, incomes, education, and aesthetic values. All of that because somebody inducted us into a polis a long time ago."

Proctor sees the problems of the young African-American male as a direct result of the failure of the African-American middle and upper classes, and the larger society as well, to "induct" these young men into the polis. He challenged members of the Task Force to "come to terms with this," and "reconcile [themselves] to the fact that they know what the issues are, but they also know where the young African-American males are; that is, young African-American males have no sense of propriety at all about this society. It is not theirs." Moreover, Proctor maintains, they have a kind of peer rating, so that their understanding of society has now become a separate subculture in and of itself, a subculture whose two primary factors, he suggests, are cynicism and fatalism.

Proctor concluded his address by posing two key questions: First, "how can we share with [young African-American males] what we have and what we enjoy to help them to get over [their cynicism and despair]?" And, second, "What would it take for us to induct all of our young people into [the polis]?"

The significance of Dr. Proctor's discussion of the Greek polis lies, not in its literal applicability to the problems of the young African-American male, but in its focus on the centrality of commonly shared values, expected and accepted behaviors, and visions of what constitutes the "good life" for a group or groups of human beings living in geographic proximity, under a given political arrangement.

Proctor's discussion is particularly acute and insightful when it highlights the time immediately following the Second World War, when the culture of the African-American community was characterized by the existence of a set of tacit, yet clearly understood values and expected and accepted behaviors. It is in this sense that the analogy of the Classical Greek polis begins to shed light on an approach to solving the problems of today's African-American young men.

Historically, the concept of the polis has operated in African-American culture as the concept of "community." Just as Aristotle argued that the polis was the third, and highest, natural evolutionary form of association (with the formation of the household and the formation of the village being its two predecessors), the African-American community is the third and highest form of association, which grew, first, out of the family; and, second, the extended family.

Just as members of the Greek polis were expected to behave in a certain way and shared a common set of values, there was a time when an identical set of conditions existed within this nation's African-American community. In fact, Dr. Proctor's idea that these values and expected behaviors were tacitly agreed upon is an accurate description of the African-American community. In the African-American community the rules were unwritten, but understood and agreed upon nonetheless.

Until very recently, there had always been a "sense of community" among African-Americans. This "sense" was evinced in innumerable ways: respect for elders; respect for authority; encouraging each other to do and be the best; pride in the accomplishments of other members of the community; mutual aid; the value of education; the value of work; the value of struggle and perseverance in the face of overwhelming odds; faith in our ability to succeed; the value of the spiritual over the material; and, perhaps most importantly, faith in a supreme being.

It was these values that helped African-Americans to survive, as a people, as a community, for more than two hundred years, from slavery to freedom, from segregation to integration. What has happened to the African-American sense of community?

Values and Community

Bazel E. Allen and Ernest J. Wilson have written in their new foreword to the 1984 publication of *The Crisis of the Negro Intellectual*: "Many of the old problems of economy and culture are still with us, and new ones have come to the surface that are, in many ways, even more perplexing and difficult to resolve. For, unseen at the time, in tandem with the long-sought gains of the Civil Rights Movement there also came *a sense of loss of community*."

The African-American polis—the community—has witnessed a radical change in fundamental values during the last decade. Yet, while this change in values became strikingly obvious only in recent years, there is evidence to suggest that many African-American intellectuals saw this change in its inchoate stages beginning in the 1950s.

In 1967, Harold Cruse quoted portions of a 1952 essay written by W. E. B. DuBois:

We must admit that the majority of American Negro intelligentsia, together with much of the West Indian and West African leadership, shows symptoms of following in the footsteps of western acquisitive society, with its exploitation of labor, monopoly of land and its resources, and with private profit for the smart and unscrupulous in a world of poverty, disease and ignorance, as the natural end of human culture. I have long noted and fought this all too evident tendency, and built my faith in its ultimate change on an inner Negro cultural ideal. I thought this ideal would be built on ancient African communism, supported and developed by memory of slavery and experience of caste, which would drive the Negro group into a spiritual unity precluding the development of economic classes and inner class struggle. This was once possible, but it is now improbable.[20]

At the time this essay was written, 1952, the United States was experiencing unprecedented economic growth as a direct result of the expansion of the American economy following the close of the Second World War. It was during this period that the U.S. Congress began to spend as though economic growth would continue forever. The private sector began putting in place overly generous pension plans, the same plans that are the impetus for much of today's restructuring of American corporate culture, from IBM to Lockheed.

It was also during this period that many mainstream American intellectuals and other thinkers began to question the fundamental values of American culture itself. Starting from the belief that "the ultimate disease of our time is valuelessness," the First Scientific Conference on New Knowledge in Human Values was held at the Massachusetts Institute of Technology (MIT), October 4 and 5, 1957. With funds provided by the Lilly Endowment, on October 29, 1955, a group of thirteen American educators and intellectuals met at Emerson Hall, Harvard University, to form the Harvard Research Center in Creative Altruism, the conference sponsor.

In his essay titled "The Powers of Creative Unselfish Love," Pitirim A. Sorokin, Professor of Sociology Emeritus, Harvard University, and one of the founding members of the Research Society wrote, in 1959:

The central reason for the establishment of the Harvard Research Center ... has been the idea that the moral transformation of man and the man-made universe is the most important item on today's agenda of history. Without moral transformation in altruistic directions, neither new world wars and other catastrophes can be prevented nor a new—better and nobler—social order be built in the human universe. Without a notable increase of what we call creative, unselfish love in man and in the human universe, all fashionable prescriptions for prevention of wars and for building a new order cannot achieve their purpose.

For instance, one such fashionable prescription is a political reconstruction of all nations along the lines of American democracy. Despite the popularity of this belief, it is questionable. Tomorrow, hypothetically, you could have all nations reconstructed politically along the lines of the American brand of democracy; and yet such a reconstruction would neither prevent nor decrease the chances of new world wars or of bloody internal revolutions Why? Because study of all the wars and important disturbances from 600 BC to the present reveals that democracies are no less belligerent, no less militant, and no more orderly than autocracies.[21]

Abraham H. Maslow, then Professor of Psychology at Brandeis University and also one of the founding members of the Research Center, is of the opinion that:

The state of valuelessness has been variously described as anomie, amorality, anhedonia, rootlessness, emptiness, hopelessness, and the lack of something to believe in and to be devoted to. It has come to its present dangerous point because all the traditional value systems ever offered to mankind have in effect proved to be failures. Furthermore, wealth and prosperity, technological advance, widespread education, democratic political forms, even honestly good intentions and avowals of good will have, by their failure to produce peace, brotherhood, serenity and happiness, confronted us even more nakedly and unavoidably with the profundities that mankind has been avoiding by its busyness with the superficial.[22]

It is important to note that at virtually the same time that the Civil Rights Movement was seeking to integrate African-Americans into mainstream society, many persons at the very pinnacle of the culture into which African-Americans sought to integrate were, themselves, seriously questioning the very fundamental values of the society itself.

The Loss of Faith and Community

One of the most important factors throughout the work on these issues of African-American men and boys has been the outstanding leadership of the men and women who work with boys in communities. Spirituality is a vital force moving within these people; even though they are seemingly on the very edge of chaos in these communities, prayers are said, blessings are asked, and God is thanked at almost every moment of intervention with both the boys and with the larger community.

James Melvin Washington, Professor of Church History at Union Theological Seminary in New York, spent twenty years researching the history of the black church in America. During his research, "he would run across a prayer in a nineteenth-century newspaper, a slave narrative or an autobiography, make a copy and save it." Eventually, Washington decided to publish his collection of prayers in a book titled, *Conversations with God: Two Centuries of Prayers by African-Americans.*[23]

Washington reached at least six major conclusions during the course of his research. First, he has noticed too many "dead people, walking around spreading death." He feels these people are suffering from what he calls "compassion fatigue"; that is, the enormous needs, violence, and drug abuse in the black community have meant that there is a shortage of people who care about what happens to those around them.

A second conclusion is that "too many African-Americans have fallen into nihilism, and have rejected religious beliefs and traditional values."

Yet, he finds it amazing that "in the face of enormous pain and deprivation there were so many black people who prayed and believed in God."

Based on the prayers he collected, Washington concluded that the most prevalent issue within African-American spirituality has been how to be a Christian in an unrighteous world, and the most common theme he found is a response to the different historical formations of the absurd.

Yet it is his fifth conclusion which is the most illuminating and seminal. Here he determined that the most absurd formation of all was the assassination of Martin Luther King, Jr. It was not King's murder *per se*, but the timing. Right after the major victories of the Voting Rights Acts of 1964 and 1965:

> *You build up all that energy, that historic steam, and suddenly you get there and the one who made you is shot. The link between the African-American confidence in the eventual goodness of democracy and the power of the Christian Church was deeply shaken. This event spiritually devastated the African-American community.* It was harder to find prayers after 1970.[24]

Finally, however, according to Washington, many African-Americans continue to hold onto their faith in God: "God is real, right here now, even though I don't understand it."

Even though it may not be well understood, it is apparent that men and women in communities, when they invest themselves in and work with these young men, find that it is their religious and spiritual beliefs that carry their programs and tend to bring and hold the boys.

Conclusion

The reestablishment of civil society is at the heart of the idea of the polis. The polis, which is nothing more than the individual working in the community, cannot be established, however, until public kinship becomes a part of the total personhood of those individuals involved in community building. In the present situation is such a kinship possible?

John S. Mbiti, expert in African religions and philosophies says:

> *Just as God made the first man, as God's man, so now a man himself makes the individual who becomes the corporate or social man. It is a deeply religious transaction. Only in terms of other people does the individual become conscious of his own being, his own duties, his privileges and responsibilities toward himself and toward other people. When he suffers, he does not suffer alone. But with the corporate group, when he rejoices, he rejoices not alone but with his kinsman, his neighbors and his relatives whether dead or living. When he gets married, he is not alone, neither does his wife "belong" to him alone. So also the children belong to the corporate body of kinsmen, even if they bear only their father's name. Whatever happens to the individ-*

ual happens to the whole group, and whatever happens to the whole group happens to the individual. The individual can only say: "I am because we are; and since we are, therefore, I am.[25]

This is a cardinal point in the understanding of the African view of man. As many African-Americans today begin to espouse this African view of man, it may be that this is simply more than an African view. It may be the universal view that humans will have to adapt if we are to remain as human beings in symbiotic relationships on this planet. However, it is a very arduous task to lay claim upon someone merely because of their skin color or their ethnic background or even their nationality. Particularly when in reality there may be no claims that you have upon that person—his actions, his values, his morals—since the corporate body does not raise this particular child.

We must do more to understand how the polis can work to create a common set of understandings, so that this principle of the polis and the hold that the polis must have upon each of us as we carry out our duties and responsibilities to both the state and to ourselves is accomplished. It is very difficult, but it is certainly a cardinal principle that must be put into place if African-American men and boys and their families and communities are to make the kinds of changes that are necessary to bring them into full participation before the turn of the century.

Attorney Don Anderson, director of the National Association for the Southern Poor has, in fact, developed such a program. It is a program that speaks to the development of the polis within communities where no such polis exists. The following excerpt from the National Center for Nonprofit Boards gives NASP's philosophy.[26]

Interview

Don Anderson's Unusual Organization Seeks To Empower Poor People at the Grass Roots

The National Association for the Southern Poor (NASP) is the brainchild of Don Anderson. Now 63, Anderson dreamed the idea when he was 14, before undergraduate and law degrees from the University of Michigan and a graduate degree from the London School of Economics. Former general counsel for the Poverty Subcommittee of the U.S. House of Representatives' Committee on Education and

Labor, he was among those who created the antipoverty programs of the 1960s. Learning from those "failures," he fashioned the NASP to organize local communities to solve their own problems. From his Washington office, Anderson answered the editor's questions about his unusual strategies for implementing social change and what these techniques may mean for all nonprofits.

Question: Where did the idea for your organization originate?

I grew up in the apartheid system of the South. We could never go to restaurants, to theaters. We existed essentially in an all black world. This was in Charlotte, North Carolina, where I lived my first 11 years. My grandfather was a slave.

As I was growing up, I remember everybody around me saying, "We've got to get organized." But nobody said how. That was left to me.

When I went to the University of Michigan I really entered the white world. I saw that the only way we blacks were going to change was by becoming organized ourselves.

The model for how to do it came to me at the London school of Economics. The model was the British House of Commons.

Question: Your group encourages local communities to solve problems by organizing small groups of citizens into Conferences and Assemblies. Explain?

The idea of the Assembly is simply a copy of the House of Commons. Our goal in every community we enter is to give local leaders the tools to organize themselves to solve their own problems. The central unit is the Assembly, made up of representatives of individual Conferences. This organizational structure connects people for the first time who have been unconnected before.

Question: Why this approach?

I was on the staff of Adam Clayton Powell. I helped draft antipoverty legislation. Then I saw its failings. I conducted the first investigation by the House of Representatives into community action programs throughout the country. In every place, I saw the same thing: people from Washington would go in and provide leadership at the local level. That's wrong. That takes the initiative away from the people of the community.

Question: Is it as true today as it was then?

Yes. We as a nation could make a terrible mistake by sending volunteers into poor rural communities to do public service. That always takes the initiative away from the community.

Question: You have devised a structure that works from the bottom up, not from the top down?

Yes, each community identifies its own problems and figures out how to solve them. The people in a community always know what their problems are. We on the outside are always completely ignorant of their problems.

An essential tenet of the National Association for the Southern Poor is that neither staff nor board will advance any ideas to a local community. We will help it organize itself and we will provide technical assistance, but the community must solve its problems itself.

Question: What is your role?

I have two roles because, in essence, we are two organizations in one. As executive director, my main responsibility is to enable the board to fulfill its governance functions. I'm in charge of the overall direction of the organization. I hire the staff and work with the corporate board, which is the public face, to raise the money. I also take an active part in the origin of each local Assembly. Then I withdraw slowly so that local citizens take over.

Question: When you go into a community, what do you do?

I speak to community leaders. I present to them the idea of the Assembly. I find the dynamics of those early meetings quite amazing. On the one hand, leaders are frustrated because they want to reach their people and can't. And the people themselves have a predisposition to organize—or to be organized—but don't know how.

When I present the idea to them, the outcome is still astounding even to me after a quarter of a century: you can almost see in their eyes the words "Eureka, this is what we have been waiting for."

Question: Who are these local leaders?

Most, almost all, are uneducated people who have gone on and done magnificent things. Usually there is no middle class. If there is, it's an impediment; the middle class has great anxieties about organizing.

Question: Does your organization provide local groups with money?

No. We only provide technical assistance. They look to us to try to find doctors to practice. We find legal assistance in dealing with county government. Housing is a good example. We're assisting communities to prepare proposals to HUD. We provide all kinds of technical assistance, but no money. The main thing we do is to help them organize themselves.

Question: Does this approach take a long time?

Sometimes. Even some of our board members expect these communities to come out of poverty in a year. "Remember," I say to them, "how close we are to slavery. I was 34 years old before I could vote in Virginia."

Question: What kinds of problems do local communities tackle?

Recreation centers, low income housing, scholarship funds, better education. Usually they start with insubstantial ideas, but once they have had minimal success—like getting a road paved—they become bold. They've brought millions of dollars into these areas.

Question: Dedicated as you are to a grassroots approach, talk about the deficiencies of federal, state, or private initiatives that are top-down programs.

Most people who try to help the poor aren't experts on helping the poor. So they offer assistance which is essentially crippling. It takes away the initiative of the poor themselves.

Question: Is this fault widespread?

Yes. Most efforts begin with a program—which is a contradiction of the premise of self-help. If you begin with a program, you begin with the idea. We, instead, begin with the structure of organization which enables the poor to create their own programs. Neither the poor—nor anyone else—can come up with a program unless there is a vehicle for engaging in collective decision making.

Question: Does that suggest that top-down programs always will fail?

Yes, unless you have some way of engaging in collective decision making by large numbers of people.

Remember Jefferson's words: "I hope they will adopt the subdivision of our counties into wards. Each ward would thus be a small republic within itself and every man in the state would thus become an active member of the common government . . . "

Question: Throughout America millions of nonprofit organizations—from the largest to the smallest—are providing a multitude of services to a multitude of constituencies. Are they an important force in our society?

I'll give you the views of the chairman of my board —which I share. He's been on many nonprofit boards. He sees these organizations spending vast amounts of money and achieving only symbolic things, millions of dollars to help only a few people. You end up having huge efforts giving rise to only symbolic results. The work does not result in the great changes our society needs. The system—our institutions—do not work.

Question: Continue.

We have a population with vast potentials. As H. G. Wells said, "How many Machiavellis and how many Mozarts are out there?" We've found some. A manual laborer from the tobacco fields of Virginia is now on the stage of the Metropolitan Opera through our efforts. Many others are doctors and lawyers. But we will lose these people if we don't change the system. We are losing the potential of our country.

Question: What's your solution?

Nonprofit organizations, like government, tend to deal with pieces of the problem. Too much money is spent on single issues. The Assemblies are not ever issue-organized. They are not directed at solving a single, specific problem. They are organized for their own sake so that these organizations can deal with whatever problems come up. We are not a single issue organization.

Question: Are you saying that fragmentation is a danger?

Unfortunately, most efforts today attack symptoms—like teenage pregnancy—instead of root problems. The way to prevent the transmission of poverty to the next generation is education. I have seen the complete transformation of counties. It gives me inspiration every time I go to some of these areas to see what we have done.

Assemblies and Conferences are the key organizational units of grassroots democracy in the strategy of the National Association for the Southern Poor (NASP). In each organized location (city or county), an Assembly guides the local effort. It is composed of leaders of local Conferences made up of fifty people each. This structure empowers local citizens to identify and solve their own problems.

The NASP has offices in Washington, D.C., Durham, North Carolina, and Atlanta, Georgia. Its work focuses on 258 poor counties in Alabama, Arkansas, Georgia, Louisiana, Mississippi, North Carolina, South Carolina, Tennessee, and Virginia. Its annual budget of $500,000 comes from foundations and individuals. Among its accomplishments:

- Construction of a high school, medical center, and recreation center in Surry County, Virginia.
- Establishment of a day care center and medical facility in Gates County, North Carolina.
- New housing for 100 families in Prince Edward County, Virgina.
- Closing of the jail in Surry County, Virginia; there is no more crime.

Venturing to assume that this polis can be created with programs like the one established by the National Association for the Southern Poor, the following recommendations are made relative to the establishment of polis or community within the African-American society:

Because the issue of the polis is very much conceptual, this section must establish at least four assumptions that should be explained:

First, in the African-American culture, the concept of the polis is analogous to the concept of community. Both concepts contain the notions of expected and accepted behaviors, in addition to a set of values agreed upon either tacitly or explicitly:

Second, for at least the last two decades, we have witnessed a loss of the sense of community among African-Americans. This loss has been replaced by a series of negative behaviors and formulations including, but not limited to, what African-American church historian James Melvin Washington calls "compassion fatigue," nihilism, and a turning away from traditional religious and spiritual values.

Third, the restoration of the African-American polis (community) is crucial to the solution of problems facing its young males, and must involve a return to traditional religious and spiritual values.

Fourth, the African-American intellectual community needs to rethink and reexamine the goals it would like the African-American community to achieve, in light of the questioning of fundamental American political, economic, and educational values by mainstream Americans at the apex of culture itself. We need to amplify our concept of "success" to include more than material achievement.

In *Habits of the Heart*, published in 1985, Robert N. Bellah and his Associates on Individualism and Commitment in American Life wrote the following:

> But the solution to our problems remain opaque because of our profound ambivalence. When times are prosperous, we do not mind a modest increase in "welfare." When times are not so prosperous, we think that at least our own successful careers will save us and our families from failure and despair. We are attracted against our skepticism, to the idea that poverty will be alleviated by the crumbs that fall from the rich man's table. The Neocapitalist ideology tells us. Some of us often feel, and most of us sometimes feel, that we are only someone if we have "made it" and can look down on those who have not. The American dream is often a very private dream of being the star, the uniquely successful and admirable one, the one who stands out from the crowd of ordinary folk who don't know how. And since we have believed in that dream for a long time and worked very hard to make it come true, it is hard for us to give it up even though it contradicts another dream that we have—that of living in a society that would really be worth living in.[27]

RECOMMENDATIONS

The Task Force recommends that:

- The work of Don Anderson and the National Association for the Southern Poor be considered by communities across the country that wish to be engaged in work to bring about a polis within their communities and that they should consult this organization on ways of using the various tools and conceptual framework that NASP uses to bring about individual commitment to the development of community.
- The Domestic Service and Opportunity Corps be established. As proposed by Dr. Steven J. Wright and with additional development by

Dr. Karen Johnson-Pitman, Dr. A. Knighton Stanley and Dr. Bobby William Austin, this program takes on the features of a domestic peace corps that would address the critical problems threatening young African-American males in the United States. It would be thoroughly researched and within a given period of time would be made operational in major cities in the United States; its focus would be on service as a way of developing policy. The involvement of historically black colleges and universities would be a major part of its development, as well as the local development of leadership within those communities in which this Domestic Service and Opportunity Corps would function.

The development of this plan with a proposal should be done immediately, allowing a number of the nation's major corporations and foundations to become partners in this comprehensive approach to reestablishing community civility.

• Local communities, working with some national organizations, create calendars or planners for boys and their families that basically attempt to structure or restructure how they use their time. Time is one of the most precious commodities that these young men have. If time is not used wisely by these boys and their parents, they will not have time when they can make changes in their lives. Critical to this task, we believe, could be the nation's superintendents of schools and the nation's national black church organizations and the nation's historically black colleges. The idea is to recapture and restructure time so that it can be used wisely and appropriately. The calendar would allow parents a tool which could be used to know where their children are and what their children are doing.

Much collaboration would be needed to create youth planners that focus on time management, so that young people get the most out of their days. They need to be able to create and be surrounded by a new voice and a vision of who they are. This will need to be established with the church, the school, and the community. A six-month funded work group should be established to create this new calendar of community. This calendar would bring together the three major institutions that are critical in the lives of young people—home, church, and school.

• A national network of youth camps be established in at least the four major regions of the United States and that this system of youth camps be geared toward teaching environmental concerns and the use of technology as a way of creating sustainable living environments for the present and the future. This youth system for urban black boys would be a way to give boys summer programs which do not exist at this time. It may be that collaboration between established institutions such as Boys Clubs and Boy Scouts and local community organizations could be developed to establish these youth camps.

• Citizenship schools, as outlined by Dr. Harry Boyte in his address to the Task Force and as they are now being implemented by the Children's Defense Fund through the Black Child Community Crusade, should be created at a renewed and vigorous level to provide what young people must have to become productive citizens within the nation. This school of grassroots democracy is essential to reinvent civic life and social institutions for young men and women in America's urban communities.

CIVIC STORYTELLING AND PUBLIC KINSHIP

*P*UBLIC kinship and civic story-
telling center around the issues of how these young men and their
ancestors fit into American culture. It raises the question of
whether the ordinary human who successfully creates public kinship is not really the hero worthy of our honor. The arts, the
humanities, and education provide the means for civic storytelling.
In the public arena, the civic story is told and retold, thus establishing one's place in the society and creating the necessary kinship. Positive images of black men in American society continue to
be elusive even though the overwhelming majority of African-
American men are positive, creative, contributing leaders in
American life. Dr. Harry Boyte brought the idea of public work and
civic storytelling to the Task Force.

Background

Dr. Jessie Carney Smith, university librarian and Cosby professor at
Fisk University, discussed some of the historical and contemporary
icons and images of the African-American male.

*Frederick Douglass noted that blacks were viewed by white
Americans as a source of amusement, not as an object to resent.*

Whenever blacks moved up the social ladder, however, Douglass noted that they were resented. Thus, a black person had to be kept in a special place—his place.

Smith found one icon, the lawn jockey particularly troublesome. She noted the mixed image it gives and recounted the story of the lawn jockey.

If we are to examine the strange ways that black men have been depicted in American culture, no point of departure could be more fitting than the image of the lawn jockey. Some African-Americans concluded that the lawn jockey was a symbol of racism and showed the black male in a servant role. This may not be why this jockey is located in someone's yard, particularly if it is a white person's yard, but that is how it was viewed by blacks. The black lawn jockey may well have been one of the most successful attempts to show stereotypical pictures of blacks to dehumanize the whole race.

There are several stories that surround the lawn jockey figure. The jockey depicts negative as well as positive views. In one story the lawn jockey was created to honor a young black boy, a courageous young man who performed a noble deed for General George Washington. As the story goes, Washington needed someone to hold his horse when he attacked the British forces on Christmas Day. Tom Graves, a black volunteer in the Continental Army, and his young son Jocko had already crossed the Delaware River. Someone asked, "Who will hold the General's horse?" Jocko stepped forward and said, "I will." This was a very cold night, and this young lad stood firmly in the line of duty holding the reins of the horses and froze to death. When the war ended, and the president was out of office, it is said he returned to Mt. Vernon and ordered the erection of a statue of Jocko Graves on the lawn of his mansion. According to some, we should honor Jocko and not ridicule him.

On the other hand, William Seibert gives another explanation of the Jocko, sometimes called the Iron Mannequin, and says that one abolitionist operated a station on the Underground Railroad and used the figure with or without a flag in its hand. This was to advertise the work that was going on. Conductors were to be influenced by the presence of the flag in the hand—the flag meaning that the station was open for passengers. . . .

The suggested association between blacks and horse racing should yield a positive image and should provide inspiration for students of African-American history. There is evidence that black jockeys played a key role in the shaping of American horse racing history. Of the fifteen riders in the inaugural Kentucky Derby, fourteen were black. Oliver Lewis rode a horse to victory in the first "Run for the Roses" held in 1875. Isaac Murphy is said to be the greatest jockey in American history. In the early years of the racing event, Murphy rode horses to win three Kentucky Derbies.

The images of blacks are all around us. Images are expressed in certain terminology, clichés, expressions, sayings, stories, and so on. They have their roots in other cultures or other American groups. Such images also distort views of early American folk life.

This issue of image is indeed a difficult one. As Dr. Smith so beautifully illustrated, in many cases the use of the image may, in fact, have kernels of truth. But it can be distorted, re-created, or reshaped to create a desired result which is meant to insult and to dehumanize. Through its discussion of images, Task Force members and representatives from various media spoke of the need to use their influence to get major media carriers and promoters to portray black men in more positive ways. While negative stereotypical images of black males seem to sell magazines, videos, and CDs, the same negative images destroy the self-concepts of thousands of young African-American boys whose only contact with another male of their own culture may be through the media, thus creating through mainstream society an attitude toward these young boys which is counterproductive to their positive growth and development, emotionally and professionally.

In a paper presented to the Task Force, Paul Martin DuBois discussed the vicious cycle of what he calls "dominant culture failure" in which he showed how hopelessness spreads to disengagement, disengagement repels more people from public life, which in turn creates structural and cultural barriers resulting in the worsening of the problem. In this sense, DuBois is talking about the dominant culture of failure within American society, but it is obvious that when young men within this society receive certain images about themselves, they too begin to withdraw from any sense of understanding of who they are in a positive sense. Repeated negative images of African-American males on television, in the media, and in musical lyrics contribute to the poor image and self-perception of many black men.

African-American Men in the Media

The image of the African-American male looks like this: Michael Jackson represents a child molester; O. J. Simpson represents a "not guilty" murderer and a wife batterer; Magic Johnson represents the specter of the disease of AIDS; Mike Tyson represents the date rapist. Oddly enough, you could add to that mixture that Colin Powell could represent an American general, and Bill Cosby a very funny and comfortable man. But what is most pervasive are the negative images of black men that have now been brought to the public arena to act as the cover story, or as one television commentator was able to say, "They focus the lens through which we see the disease." That is, one sees how awful spousal abuse is, the resulting murder, and how badly justice is rendered, through the O. J. Simpson trial.

On the other hand, Susan Smith of South Carolina, who murdered her children over a lost love (and blamed that murder on a black man), does not have a national image as a child killer. Nor does it appear that Charles Stuart, who murdered his wife in Boston and caused a whole community of black men to be searched by police, based on his calculated story that a black man had robbed and murdered her, became a symbol of wife killers. Both of these individuals knew that it was all right to play the race card in the public arena. It was acceptable in the public psyche to regard a black man as the dark predator, a representative of a violence-prone people. It is no mistake that these two individuals sought to shift the burden of blame for their wickedness upon black men, because it is something that the entire white society would not only believe, but have absolutely no trouble believing.

On the other hand, it is obvious that an equally contentious state exists between black men and boys and their mothers and girlfriends when one listens to the rap music of this generation of young people. The lyrics express better than anyone ever could the hostility, the anger that these young men have toward their mothers and women in general. Once you see this situation, this explosive anger, which is the leading influence on rap music and its violent offspring, gangster rap, the world view of the young men who spew this venom is understandable, if not acceptable. Even though major women's organizations have taken them to task for their lyrics, they continue to produce them. It is important to criticize gangster rap. It is also important to try to understand from whence it comes.

Once again, it is the position of the Task Force that the only way to eliminate the hostility and hatred in this music is to find a way to bring peace to this particular segment of the African-American community. However, those who produce such media presentations, including movies, television, and the record industry, could go a long way in easing the pain and the burden of this group of young men by not repeating a story which is not a healthy civic story, because as this story is told and retold, it tends to be seen as a fact.

James Baldwin says, "Society is held together by our need. We're binded together with legend, myth, coercion, fearing that without it we will be hurled into that void within which, like the earth before the Word was spoken, the foundations of society are hidden."[28] This is important, because things are created through word, deed, and action, and the retelling of these stories in the public life can re-create truth and symbols. That is what Gerbner and Boyte forcefully told the Task Force. But, if we wish to have the appropriate images held about a group, since individuals are represented to one another in society through group stereotypes, the only way that we can conquer this is to grab hold of it and create our own image.

We can only do this if we are prepared to deal with yet another set of factors, and for that we turn to a theory that was developed in the 1950s regarding race relations in the United States.

Race Relations as a Sense of Group Position

A paper presented by Dr. Herbert Blumer at the dedication of the Robert E. Park Building at Fisk University in March 1955, appears in the book, *Race Relations, Problems and Theorys: Essays in Honor of Robert E. Park*. Blumer states in his thesis, "Race relations exist basically in a sense of group position rather than in a set of feelings which members of one racial group have toward the members of another racial group." He goes on to say that this different way of viewing race and prejudice shifts study analysis from a preoccupation with feelings of individuals to concern with the relationship of racial groups. This is very important, because in American society today, many people do not believe and cannot see that they are prejudiced.

What Blumer does is to "shift scholarly treatment away from individual lines of experience and focus interest on the collective process by which a racial group comes to define and redefine another racial group." This is extremely important in understanding why African-American men and boys are placed in such visible positions within the American media for public scrutiny. This is not to deny that they have become media celebrities, performers, or whatever. The media simply continue to tell the story about them. The problem is that in a racially divided society where prejudice abounds it takes on a whole different connotation.

> It is crucially important to recognize that the sense of group position is not a mere summation of the feelings of position such as might be developed independently by separate individuals as they come to compare themselves with given individuals of the subordinate race. The sense of group position refers to the position of group to group, not to that of individual to individual. . . .
>
> An analysis of how the sense of group position is formed should start with a clear recognition that it is an historical product. It is set originally by conditions of initial contact. . . Subsequent experience in the relation of the two racial groups, especially in the area of claims, opportunities, and advantages, may mold the sense of group position in many diverse ways. . . .
>
> However variable its particular career, the sense of group position is clearly formed by a running process in which the dominant racial group is led to define and redefine the subordinate racial group and the relations between them . . . .
>
> The implications of the fact that the collective image is of an abstract group are of crucial significance. I would like to note four of these implications.
>
> First, the building of the image of the abstract group takes place in the area of the remote and not of the near. It is not the experience with concrete individuals in daily association that gives rise to the definitions of the extended, abstract group. Such immediate experience is limited to the individuals involved. The collective image of the abstract group grows up not by generalizing from experiences gained in close, first-hand contacts but through the transcending characterizations that are made of the group as an entity. Thus, one must seek the central stream of definition in those areas where the dominant

group as such is characterizing the subordinate group as such. This occurs in the "public arena" wherein the spokesmen appear as representatives and agents of the dominant group. The extended public arena is constituted by such things as legislative assemblies, public meetings, conventions, the press, and the printed word. What goes on in this public arena attracts the attention of large numbers of the dominant group and is felt as the voice and action of the group as such.

Second, the definitions that are forged in the public arena center, obviously, above matters that are felt to be of major importance. Thus, we are led to recognize the crucial role of the "big event" in developing a conception of the subordinate racial group. The event that seems momentous, that touches deep sentiments, that seems to raise fundamental questions about relations, and that awakens strong feelings of identification with one's racial group is the kind of event that is central in the formation of the racial image. Here, again, we note the relative unimportance of the huge bulk of experiences coming from daily contact with individuals of the subordinate group. It is the events seemingly loaded with great collective significance that are the focal points of the public discussion. The definition of these events is chiefly responsible for the development of a racial image and of the sense of group position. When this public discussion takes the form of a denunciation of the subordinate racial group, signifying that it is unfit and a threat, the discussion becomes particularly potent in shaping the sense of social position.

Third, the major influence in public discussion is exercised by individuals and groups who have the public ear and who are felt to have standing, prestige, authority, and power. Intellectual and social elites, public figures of prominence, and leaders of powerful organizations are likely to be the key figures in the formation of the sense of group position and in the characterization of the subordinate group. It is well to note this in view of the not infrequent tendency of students to regard race prejudice as growing out of the multiplicity of experiences and attitudes of the bulk of the people.

Fourth, we also need to perceive the appreciable opportunity that is given to strong interest groups in directing the lines of discussion and setting the interpretations that arise in such discussion. Their self-interest may dictate the kind of position they wish the dominant racial group to enjoy. It may be a position which enables them to retain cer-

tain advantages or, even more, to gain still greater advantages . . . .

I conclude this highly condensed paper with two further observations that may throw additional light on the relation of the sense of group position to race prejudice. Race prejudice becomes entrenched and tenacious to the extent the prevailing social order is rooted in the sense of social position. This has been true of the historic South in our country. In such a social order race prejudice tends to become chronic and impermeable to change. In other places the social order may be affected only to a limited extent by the sense of group position held by the dominant racial group. This I think has been true usually in the case of anti-Semitism in Europe and this country. Under these conditions the sense of group position tends to be weaker and more vulnerable. In turn, race prejudice has a much more variable and intermittent career, usually becoming pronounced only as a consequence of grave disorganizing events that allow for the formation of a scapegoat.

This leads me to my final observation which in a measure is an indirect summary. The sense of group position dissolves and race prejudice declines when the process of running definition does not keep abreast of major shifts in the social order. When events touching on relations are not treated as "big events" and hence do not set crucial issues in the arena of public discussion; or when the elite leaders or spokesmen do not define such big events vehemently or adversely, or where they define them in the direction of racial harmony; or when there is a paucity of strong interest groups seeking to build up a strong adverse image for special advantage—under such conditions the sense of group position recedes and race prejudice declines.

The clear implication of my discussion is that the proper and the fruitful area in which race prejudice should be studied is the collective process through which a sense of group position is formed. Race prejudice has a history, and the history is collective. To seek, instead, to understand it or to handle it in the arena of individual feeling and of individual experience seems to me to be clearly misdirected.[29]

It was important to provide a major portion of the text of this theory. Blumer's discussion of the big event is particularly important given the recent trial of O. J. Simpson. Once an issue is made a big event, that one event can serve to define the subordinate group. Once created, it can be a story of sympathy or it could be a story of profound prejudice and racism.

This is, in fact, where Peter Senge's systems-change model comes into full effect. Senge identifies the event as the tip of the iceberg, meaning that two-thirds of the issue rests below the surface. The big event may be publication of *The Bell Curve: Intelligence and Class Structure in the United States*, by Herrnstein and Murray, in 1995. This book caused major controversy as a big event. It followed all of the steps enunciated in the development of group position as stated by Blumer. The collective image of the group has pretty much been established over three hundred years, and the African-American in general is almost public property in regards to public policy and discussion of his development and his career as a social being in the United States.

Therefore, the first step of the abstract image was present. Onec we see that an issue has moved to the public arena, the spokesman, in this instance the author of the book, becomes a representative of a particular point of view. This is then given to the press within the public arena to use in any way they see fit, and of course, it is about the abstract "other group." The big event, of course, could be violence, could be murder, could be any event that causes people to resonate around racially tied issues. The key figures, then, begin either to act as witnesses for this in public discussion, or to provide the discussion in which it takes place.

For instance, an article regarding the relationship between foundations and *The Bell Curve*, by Leslie Lenkowsky, appearing in the November 29, 1994 issue of the *Chronicle of Philanthropy*, asserts that, "Grant makers should consider the implications for philanthropy of the controversial book, *The Bell Curve*, rather than consigning it to the oblivion its critics claim it deserves." Lenkowsky, president of the Hudson Institute, theorizes that:

> *Philanthropy's core commitment to improving social conditions in order to improve human welfare implies a conviction, perhaps not always articulated, that if given the opportunity, people can change significantly, not least of all in cognitive functioning. If people could not change, the best course would seem to be to provide simple charity for the less fortunate—a calling that most modern philanthropists reject out of hand.*
>
> *The evidence presented by Richard J. Herrnstein and Charles Murray in* The Bell Curve *calls that conviction into question. As the authors report, the consensus view is that a large share—40 to 80 per-*

cent—of how much intelligence a person has comes by way of inheritance. Moreover, intelligence appears to have an enormous effect on what a person is able to do, from the ability to earn income to the likelihood of becoming a criminal or a teen-age mother. In view of that, the prospect that philanthropic endeavors can make much difference in changing the lives of people with lesser ability would seem to be grim.

It is important to note that numerous critics have called this work unscientific, particularly since the thesis of the book centers on genetics and both authors are social scientists—not geneticists.

Nevertheless, with this kind of "big event," one can create the atmosphere wherein change occurs without real insight, spurred on by dubious science and the public dialogue that can ensue from it.

The proof of group position and image can be found in a recent national telephone survey sponsored by the Washington Post, the Kaiser Family Foundation, and Harvard University. The headline in the October 8, 1995, Washington Post says it all: "A Distorted Image of Minorities." The conclusions garnered from this survey are that (a) Americans do not know each other; (b) we harbor suspicions about each other; and (c) we rely on myths about each other, consequently developing distorted images about the "other" group.

Media and Image

Dr. George Gerbner discussed with the Task Force the relationship between African-American men and the nation's media. His discussion centered on three areas; (1) mythology and myth making; (2) the marketability of violence; and (3) the global media.

Gerbner defined the global myth making in the following way:

Our children cannot imagine, and many of our parents and very soon our grandparents, what that world was like and that is the world BT—Before Television. My task is in setting the stage for a discussion in this nation on these issues. I know you are going to discuss the business of images and imagery and what they reveal, and how to cope with them, much of the rest of this afternoon. For the first time in human history a child is born into a home in which television is on an average of seven hours and forty-one minutes a day. It's not a medium—it's an environment into which our children are born. For the first time in our history, most of the stories to most of the children most of the time are no longer told by the parent. They are not hand-crafted in the community, no longer by the school, no longer by the church, and very often no longer by anybody who really has anything to tell, but increasingly by a highly centralized, globalized group of conglomerates that have something to sell. It is impossible to over-estimate the effect that this transformation of our mythology, which is all the stories that we tell and we hear, determined in the way in which our children are socialized. A ten-year-old child today knows more brands of names of beer than names of American presidents.[30]

So shocked were Task Force members that a gasp was heard in the Appleton Room of Jubilee Hall at Fisk.

Gerbner went on to discuss with the group the marketability of violence. The answer for the pervasiveness of media violence domestically and globally is that it travels well on the global market. He explained: An American producer of television programs and of most motion pictures doesn't break even on the domestic market because there are only a few buyers and very little competition. Television has no box office. It is supported by advertisers and governments who buy the programs wholesale. If you are producing for the world market, you have to ask yourself, what is it that needs no translation—that is essentially image driven, that speaks action in any language, that can easily be introduced into the culture of almost any country? The answer to that is violence—violence then becomes an ingredient in a global marketing formula that is imposed on the creative people in Hollywood and pushed on the children of the world with global distribution of power regardless of the fact that it is not particularly popular in any country. What the producers and the syndicates lose by selling a product that is not very popular, they more than make up for it by extending the market globally and dominating the world market.

We dominate more than 50 percent of the screens of the world. These more than make up for the domestic loss by the number of countries to which violence can be sold relatively cheaply—it, in fact, presents an irresistible business deal. They say, "We can sell you one hour's worth of this programming for less money than it would cost you to produce one minute of your own.[31]

And, finally he went on to discuss with the Task Force the

effect of world media domination and the lack of response to it.

> *We have an invisible Ministry of Culture that has never been elected, whose name we don't even know unless we read the trade papers, that determines about 85 percent of what the children of the world will see, and determines it without accountability to the people.[32]*

The distorted image of the black man may, in fact, rise with how those who control media wish to portray him.

You can see, then, how big events and the global reach of media to create myths and images cannot be ignored. All are powerful tools within the public arena even if they are offered up innocently. They can be distorted, as all images can, to create the desired result. This happens particularly in a multi-racial society with a history and a career of ambivalence, hatred, and prejudice.

Public Works and Civic Storytelling

The tradition of citizenship and polis, that which in American history has often been called the commonwealth, must be revived. This was the advice offered to the Task Force by Dr. Harry Boyte of the Hubert H. Humphrey Center for Democracy and Citizenship. According to Boyte,

> *the citizenship school tradition and the tradition of the commonwealth should be renewed and needs to be renewed by a campaign for citizenship schools in the nineties and secondly by a process that's kind of a movement to make visible the civic stories, the stories of public work and public action and public genius of ordinary people in America's communities across the country which is really an invisible story, but has the possibility of giving the country new hope and a sense of promise. Then the big event would be how well we work together and how we share a common bond rather than the divisive group position and media hype of the present.[33]*

Dr. John Perkins, publisher of *Urban Family*, has begun to model the behavior of one who is engaged in public work. He is calling attention to what he calls Real Urban Role Models. Each year in his magazine, Perkins profiles twenty-five grassroots heroes and leaders. This "spotlights people of character whose lifestyles are worth emulating. These role models are not people doing good from a distance; they are the live bodies our children see and touch every day."[34]

Boyte has developed seven principles of public work.[35] He defines them in this way:

1. *Public work is the story of nonviolence and human dignity. It's a story of the contributions everyday people can make to the commonwealth. It is the dignity of ordinary labor. The commonwealth is built on the notion of public work by everybody. It is to be creative. It is to be held accountable for your work.*

2. *Public work is a mix of people. Part of the problem with our society is that everything has become so personalized, and we think everybody's got to like each other to deal with each other, or we've got to agree with each other, but the story of public work is that you learn to work with people who you don't agree with.*

3. *Doing public work, you develop craft and pride in your work, and you develop skills for work. This is the lesson of the civil rights citizenship school tradition as a whole, learning from our experience, developing a craft of politics as everyday experience. We think of citizenship as simply being born into it—we're not. Citizenship is public work. It is something you develop.*

4. *Public work is visible. It is civic storytelling, where ordinary people do extraordinary things for each other and community.*

5. *Public work is the way to think about professional and expert knowledge. The only way that's going to happen is for people who are in government to see themselves as citizens, whether they are in elected positions of power or civil servants. We must learn to work with people, not do things for them. This applies to professionals and the persons who serve the public. Putting experts on tap, not on top, and in the process, getting back to the notion of our institutions becoming public spaces, civic institutions.*

6. *The great problem today is that people do not have criteria for judging what's fair and unfair. Every group feels like it's been badly treated. If every group thinks that they're being treated unfairly, appeals to justice fall on deaf ears. When you're doing public work together, it creates a focus and seriousness, and ties the struggle for justice to a project of building together. It creates a very different flavor to it. People are able to hear each other, and listen to each others' stories of injustice, deprivation, suffering, and oppression—much more easily understood when they feel they're doing work together.*

7. When people do public work, they develop a sense of self, skills, and accountability.

RECOMMENDATIONS

The Task Force recommends that:

• A center be established for the development of media production, which would include film, recordings, and drama. This center would develop those civic stories that could be placed in the canon of stories that are told to young boys within our society. This media center would create original movies, dramas for film, and recordings that could be used in households, as well as for general marketing purposes. Further, this center would have some relationship with the nation's historically black colleges and universities.

• A national historic areas project be established that would encourage communities and families to plan visits for these boys to national historic monuments, parks, houses, and museums within the United States which specifically reference African-Americans.

• A nationwide library program for boys be developed. The strategy would be to increase the use of public libraries by African-American males, which would in turn open the door of knowledge about themselves and their culture to the rest of the world.

• An international summit on African-American men be convened which would look at their image worldwide and how that image is distributed, studied, and discussed. The Task Force recommends that programs be developed which would provide opportunities for black males to interact with positive role models and to actively participate in activities that would enhance their ability to think positively of themselves and others.

• Community centers be created with linkages to existing parts of the community that give boys opportunities to: (1) participate and to succeed; (2) get early and frequent messages about what is important and the responsible role of fathers in families; (3) participate in work programs with African-American men to develop positive work skills; and (4) develop a sense of caring for themselves and, in turn, caring for others. Each community would, where necessary, establish parenting programs for teen mothers and fathers.

• Where possible, young black men be encouraged to participate in cable television in their local areas, telling their own stories. Some education must take place for parents and individuals in communities so that they are able to become conversant with and use cable television for skill-building and to develop educational programs for adults and children. Television cannot be ignored. It will continue to play a critical role in the development of young people, but communities will have to become more involved in television as a way of protecting and educating their children.

• Collaboration should occur between universities and community colleges and community groups and organizations to create a handbook and/or a skill-building tool to use cable television as an educational tool.

• A defined "circuit" using various community theaters and auditoriums already in existence in the nation's urban centers, as well as elementary and high schools in major cities, would work out a multi-year schedule so that art and theater can be brought to boys in their communities and in their homes, and also for them to participate in the creation of their own theater and art. This could be implemented by individuals who are involved in the theatrical and artistic communities.

Sororities and fraternities could make arts and the theater a major program in which art exhibitions and theatrical productions could be produced. Suggested institutions would include the black colleges and black churches as prime venues. Also, the media center which was proposed by the television and movie workshop of the Task Force would be a major instrument in the production end of this work.

There could be many collaborators in this, for there are many community arts institutions, ballet companies, dance schools, and theatrical companies across the country that, if the appropriate setting was established, could develop these theatrical and art exhibitions for communities throughout the country. Therefore, at some future date, a national meeting should be organized which would bring these organizations and groups together to discuss such a recommendation.

• A national classical music program be established for children and young men in the African-American community. This would have, as its base, several touring professionals who would appear in various cities and do master workshops with children of all ages to teach them the structure, form, and development of music, essentially how music is created, and more specifically, to help children understand how vital their musical heritage is to the establishment of American culture and their position in that culture. Because music is such a vital part of the lives of young African-Americans, it is suggested that they be given a broader view of music and how the development of music has worked in the development of the African-American community.

This could be implemented by one or more conductors and musicians, paid to criss-cross the nation to create these forums. It could be done on local television stations, in elementary and secondary schools, high schools, colleges, and in any civic social institution in the community. This could be a major program that could galvanize a new kind of civic participation within our urban areas.

• A program of public history be established for young African-Americans in the United States. This public history program would include the use of scholars and museum experts to bring to life the history of African-Americans in the United States and their relationship to American culture. This public history project could be the basis for helping African-American boys understand the context of African-Americans in American society. There should be more practical ways of sharing the heritage of local community heroes with African-American youngsters. This is a vital and needed program. Public history would not only inform these young people; it would help to provide new civic stories for the general population at large.

• In the very near future, a task force should be established which would bring together scholars and museum professionals to develop a program of local public history for local communities, that can be implemented by local people at a local level. A community would work with local historians, not necessarily to create a national message, but to create a local public program that young people could learn from and understand regarding their history within the community.

• A book and film list be created for boys, which would be specific to educational levels. Books, perhaps in paperback form, as well as films, could be provided to libraries and community centers or public housing projects, which would allow boys to read and view the best that American culture has to offer. This series would examine the classics of American literature, including all Americans as a way of broadening perspective and understanding various cultural groups. It would be geared specifically to young children in the elementary grades. These books and films would be a major project in which the text would be written very simply to tell the story, and using accompanying film to visualize that story. A series of morality tales would be a part of such a series, and a booklet that would allow the reader to grasp relationships between individuals in the country, so that hatred recedes and a tolerance is built, showing the relationships between African-Americans and other racial and ethnic groups in the country.

GRASSROOTS CIVIC LEADERSHIP: Taking Charge in Communities

6

GRASSROOTS civic leadership is the empowering of individuals—parents, teachers, ministers, young people—to take control of their lives and communities. Programs to reinvent civil and economic life must be developed. In this chapter, the idea of individual learning paths is talked about as a way of developing personal mastery and individual capacity. Emphasis is placed upon building relationships between men and women and upon collaborative leadership, fellowship, and spiritual values.

The development of grassroots leadership and local programs is critical to bringing about fundamental improvements for African-American men and boys in urban areas. Many of the problems facing these young men are most acute at the grassroots level, including unemployment, low school achievement, and violence. It is grassroots leaders who are most likely to begin the creation of the systems changes that must take place for these young men. Grassroots civic leadership relies on cultural and spiritual leadership to bring about effective change in the community. There is every reason to believe that in cultivating grassroots leadership, African-American males do have the resources and the determination to begin taking full control of their lives. However, such public issues as economic development, the educational offerings within schools and communities, and the funding for youth initiatives that create self-reliance and entrepreneurial venues for young men are monumental. They can be tackled with the development of programs that focus on self-esteem, spirituality, and value clarification, which are a major part of what civic grassroots leadership is all about.

The overriding goal for grassroots leadership must be to enhance the work of those individuals engaged in building citizen-ship within the polis. Democracy must become a working formula so that people create for themselves a new vision that is both whole-some and self-fulfilling. Just as negatives are said to build negative reactions and poise persons for failure, a positive reengagement and understanding that citizenship is something that must be worked at would have positive results. The Task Force thought that exercising individual duty and responsibility to create this new engine of enthusiasm, no matter what one's economic position, could help positive, creative, community-building in these poor and devastated communities.

It must be obvious that no one can or should go into these communities to do for people what only they can do for themselves and what they wish to do for themselves. However, the larger com-munity does have a responsibility in the social contract to facilitate, to act as backup, and to carry on a parallel conversation with the broader community while grassroots leadership has time to form and to understand the kind of work that must be done.

Background

Too often the views and ideas of local community members are missing from public dialogue. This tends to be particularly true when it comes to developing programs for our youth. After speaking with some young men in the Washington, D.C. area, George Ayers, a Task Force member, reported that these young black males felt that African-American leaders and other concerned adults did not listen to them. They were frustrated by what they perceived to be a lack of understanding and communication on the part of those working to improve conditions in the black community.

Committee reports, formal papers, and dialogues all indicated that bridging the communication gap between middle-class profes-sional blacks and grassroots community citizens is crucial if effec-tive, long-term solutions are to be implemented in local communi-ties. Without the full support and participation of local residents, no program for positive change can hope to have a lasting success. And such programs can only be successful by empowering grassroots leadership and local community members with the skills and resources needed to control their destinies.

By generating more grassroots civic participation, we would be increasing local residents' sense of their stake in and ownership of any programs that take place in the community. This sense of ownership and involvement undoubtedly creates better possibilities for developing successful and enduring community programs.

It is important that we do not overemphasize the negative aspects of the status of African-American men and boys. Although, for example, the black poverty rate is far too high, it does not negate the fact that a great majority of African-Americans do not live in poverty. In addition, of this majority there are substantial numbers of African-American males in the middle and upper-middle class.

There are black males participating and distinguishing themselves at virtually every level of American society. And whereas it would be false to minimize the great and multiple problems confronting African-American males, it would also be wrong to undervalue the substantial achievements that black males have made and continue to make in our society. By doing so, we fall into the same kind of errors we criticize much of the media for committing: focusing only on the negative aspects of African-American males. Instead we (and the media) should give greater prominence to the significant successes of African-American males. These positive examples should be used as models to inspire young African-American men and boys with the belief that they too can succeed in their communities and in the larger community.

This kind of affirmative emphasis is consistent with Gerbner's analysis of positive and negative mythologies in our society. Part of the negative mythology for black males, as Gerbner shows, is the manner in which TV news and other media present a distorted and statistically disproportionate image of African-American males who engage in violence, who use drugs, and who are arrested. On the other hand, disproportionately less coverage is given to African-American males who are, for example, successful businessmen, lawyers, educators, scientists, and doctors in their respective communities. We must, therefore, encourage the hopes and dreams of young African-American men and boys by fostering a more positive mythology to highlight the many and varied accomplishments of African-American males.

In this context, there is an urgent need at the grassroots level to promote among African-American men and boys a greater respect for oneself and for others. This need is perhaps greatest in the area of encouraging young black males to adopt nonviolent approaches to resolving conflicts. Conflict resolution as a skill should be required in all inner-city educational institutions. More generally, a greater sense of self-respect and respect for others would help to create growing respect for and pride in the neighborhood and the wider community.

Black Church Leadership

The black church should be a leading institution in promoting self-respect for others and a communal concern for the neighbor. Throughout African-American history, as numerous black church historians have pointed out, the black church has promoted not only the spiritual development of African-Americans but the social and political development as well. There is no institution in the African-American community more grassroots than the black church. It is owned and operated by local community members and responds to the needs of the local membership. But as noted in the Washington, D.C., Focus Groups Report, the black church must become more engaged in promoting the social, political, and economic well-being of African-American men and boys. Like Martin Luther King, Jr., the church must use its ministry as an instrument for social justice.

As an independent institution within its community, the black church should be a leader in such efforts as developing educational programs, providing venture capital for black youth, and sponsoring community forums on issues of local importance. With its collective resources the black church can be a pivotal force in establishing and helping others to establish black business in the community and, thereby, increasing job opportunities. (Spiritual leadership for grassroots civic leaders will be discussed later in this chapter).

A point repeatedly made throughout the various Task Force Groups was the imperative need for African-American males in much greater numbers to become owners and operators and producers, not just consumers. Such economic development creates a firm basis upon which African-American men and boys can gain the greater self-respect and community concern discussed earlier.

As this report suggests, the needs and problems faced by African-American males is great. It is important to note, however, that throughout the country various programs are being implemented to improve the status of black men and boys. For example, the Congress of National Black Churches has programs that help to reduce violence in urban communities. In Indianapolis, a group called the One Hundred Black Men regularly sit in on the editorial board meetings of local newspapers to ensure more accurate and fairer coverage of African-American males. Youth leadership councils are being organized in Detroit so that the opinions and ideas of the youth will be reflected in programs geared towards them.

It is also important that grassroots leadership be allowed to express itself in relationship to the political forces of the particular areas because this leadership must deal with social, economic, and political issues. There can be very little economic development in these communities without a relationship with the political forces of these communities.

Therefore, grassroots civic leadership must be trained to be well-rounded, to be able to think as systems thinkers, to see the whole system and how the parts work together by using cultural and spiritual leadership skills, and to be able to create positive gains for their community and themselves as they attempt to restructure the dynamics that are now devastating these communities.

One of the most creative grassroots leadership groups in the country is MAD Dads. MAD Dads, which is a national organization formed in Omaha, Nebraska, is simply a group of men who, by virtue of their initiative, have become leaders in the streets of their communities. In these communities these men act as father figures, mentors, leaders, father confessors, and strict disciplinarians. They are, in fact, engaging young men and bringing them back to their senses simply by their presence on the streets between the hours of midnight and early morning. In these moments, these men transform the streets of their community into caring, sensitive, orchestrated workshops held on the streets.

It is this kind of grassroots leadership combating the problem head-on in the streets that will answer the questions regarding young boys and violence.

Two additional programs which develop grassroots community leadership are the Citizens Planning and Housing Association in Baltimore, Maryland, and the Neighborhood College in Hampton, Virginia.

Joyce Smith is a community leader in Baltimore's Franklin Square neighborhood. She has served as the volunteer president of the Franklin Square Community Association, an association which represents a community of approximately 3,000 people. She is currently the Association's Executive Director. One way in which Joyce has developed her leadership skills is by participating in a range of programs offered by Citizens Planning and Housing Association (CPHA) a Baltimore-based citizens organization which is dedicated to strengthening neighborhoods through leadership development, technical assistance, and coalition building. One program in particular, CPHA's Leadership Development Initiative, has helped Joyce and a team of Franklin Square leaders enhance their leadership skills, gain knowledge of and access to a range of community resources, and form networks with other community leaders. Through the leadership initiative, leaders such as Joyce receive support in organizational development, community mobilization, and community planning. In 1995, she was elected to the CPHA Board of Governors, the organization's policy body. She was nominated to the board because of her knowledge of community issues and her ability to get things done, and because she is always asking how she can change things.

The Neighborhood College in Hampton, Virginia, describes its work in the following way:

> Hampton's Neighborhood College trains neighborhood leaders, community partners, and city staff in the art of partnership and resourcefulness. One of only a handful of such training programs in the country, Hampton's Neighborhood College is unique because it extends beyond just a city/neighborhood partnership—it offers students a "how-to" tap, a full range of community resources (including each other) and creates new structure for building neighborhood health.
>
> The five-week college offers a range of courses such as "City Hall: Behind the Scenes," "Neighborhood-School Connections," "Youth and Adult Partnerships," and a tour of Hampton's neighborhoods called "Diversity in Your Backyard." A key feature of the curriculum is "homework" in building partnerships. As a graduation requirement, students do hands-on learning by actually establishing relationships with community agencies. The choice of "homework assignments" ranges from riding in a patrol car with a police officer to meeting with a school principal or attending another neighborhood's association meeting.
>
> "Certainly increasing the extent and effectiveness of civic involvement is a key objective of the Neighborhood College," says

Neighborhood Office Director, Joan Kennedy. "But the added twist in Hampton's approach is to stretch the concept of involvement beyond neighborhoods becoming more effective at communicating needs to city government. Our neighborhoods will develop a broad base of resources (inside and outside the neighborhood) to meet their own vision for a healthy neighborhood." . . .

In order to tap the resources of graduates and offer continuous support and networking opportunities, the Neighborhood College has an alumni association. Two regular college sessions are offered in the spring and fall. A Youth Leadership School, a Non-Profit Board Development School, and a Crime Prevention School are being developed as well as graduate seminars on skill topics such as neighborhood planning or grantsmanship.[36]

Cultural Leadership

Grassroots leadership can take at least two forms, one cultural and the other spiritual. When one hears the word cultural, there are many ideas that come to mind, and yet it may be that none of these are appropriate for the specific task of bringing about a new relationship and a new vision for African-American men and boys in the American context. It is essential that there be some new models and a renewed vision that can lead to discussion, and that will provide the impetus for a change in both the tone and tenor of the present American dialogue with respect to those issues and questions that are being raised in this report. Here cultural means engaging differences, through actions that bring race and class together in society through the arts, humanities, recreational sports, and social life.

George Washington Carver is the historic figure who can focus our discussion of leadership.

Carver really does not precisely fit into any of the espoused models of leadership of John Gardner, Greenleaf, or Burns; actually, he embodies the best of all of these: vision, voice, virtue, care, commitment, continuing self-development, and establishment of community. It is obvious from the discussions that any leadership paradigms will need all of these if they are to be successful.

Carver was a cultural leader and a grassroots leader. He worked at the community level breaking down racial and cultural barriers through his creation of positive relations with southern whites. He sought out ways to create kinship and he sought to blend good works with acute cultural sensitivity. Carver lived an innovative, collaborative, facilitative life. He provided the germination of ideas and vision, which he shared without thought for personal gain, because he understood community. Booker T. Washington relates a moving story about Carver. He says,

> One of the most interesting and valuable instances of the kind that I know is presented in the case of Mr. George W. Carver, one of our instructors in agriculture at Tuskegee Institute. For some time, it has been his custom to prepare articles containing information concerning the condition of local crops and warning the farmers against the ravages of certain insects and diseases. The local white papers are always glad to publish these articles, and they are read by white and colored farmers.
>
> Some months ago a white landholder in Montgomery County asked Mr. Carver to go through his farm with him for the purpose of inspecting it. While doing so, Mr. Carver discovered traces of what he thought was a valuable mineral deposit used in making a certain kind of paint. The interest of the landowner and the agricultural instructor at once became mutual. Specimens of the deposits were taken to the laboratories of the Tuskegee Institute and analyzed by Mr. Carver. In due time the landowner received the report of the analysis, together with the statement showing the commercial value and application of the mineral. I shall not go through the whole interesting story except to say that a stock company composed of the best white people in Alabama has been organized and is now preparing to build a factory for the purpose of putting that product on the market. I hardly need to add that Mr. Carver has been freely consulted at every step and his service is generously recognized in the organization of the concern. When the company was being formed, the following testimonial, among others, was embodied in the printed copy of the circular: "George Washington Carver, Director of the Department of Agriculture, Tuskegee, Alabama."
>
> Even though there are many ways people will interpret such a paragraph, don't lose sight of the spirit of Carver himself. Carver, you see, worked to create new opportunities for collaborative action by planting the seed in others. He assisted farmers, both black and white, in finding new ways to improve themselves and their crops. It is a value we all should share: doing all that we can to institutionalize, in organizations and individuals, the shared responsibility to assist with-

out thought of remuneration or praise. Throughout his long and distinguished career, George Washington Carver clearly created or developed innovative approaches to literally hundreds of products. For himself, he only sought patents for less than 25.[37]

We are in the midst of a critical period in our nation's history, both as a people and, specifically, with regard to African-American men and boys. Currently, we are celebrating a new approach to pluralism called "diversity." Still, it is apparent that diversity without common vision and shared values that lead toward common good only provides a wedge that will, in fact, weaken our common life. The leadership that springs from the Task Force, and from the spirit of George Washington Carver, finds its truth in transcultural, transracial leadership and thought, in shared values, and in the common good, all of which lead to the sharing of a common culture in which all citizens contribute to the development of society. Only with such leadership can we, as a nation, find ways to turn the tide among the nation's underclass. Only with such leadership will we find the tools and the skills to bring a new vision to that portion of African-American men and boys who are so critically in need.

This radical new public kinship must be at the very core of all that we seek to do. Consequently, we must to find those projects and personalities that can radically change the frame of reference from which we view and understand the problems and the possibilities of African-American men and boys who today are in social isolation, and in need of renewed vistas of hope.

Cultural leadership defined in the terms and vision of George Washington Carver can begin the necessary cultural dialogue that will be needed to unravel this situation, particularly at the grassroots level. A critical part of that cultural leadership paradigm will be the use of systemic thinking.Cultural and grassroots leadership must be effective on at least three levels: (1) to help individuals in all communities refashion their insights and approaches to other people who are different from themselves; (2) to help facilitate dialogue between various civic and social groups in the country; and (3) to provide a common arena for discussion and thereby create a shared vision and genuine understanding.

Spiritual Leadership

Even though we have spoken about the church there is one other area of grassroots leadership that is extremely important.

Throughout this entire process of work with African-American men and boys it has been obvious that spiritual development and spirituality have been key to the men and women who work in these areas. Consequently, we must say something about spiritual leadership.

Spiritual leadership is one aspect that can be easily linked to the work of grassroots leaders. Spiritual leadership is something that grassroots leaders, as well as many other leaders, do. As described by Parker Palmer, the celebrated visionary, spiritual leadership is must involve an inward voyage into one's own inner being and soul. Good leaders do this in order that they can come to the world with a new sense of morality, humanness, and vision. This inward journey, Palmer tells us, can be profound.

> *A leader is a person who has an unusual degree of power to create the conditions under which other people must live and move and have their being—conditions that can either be as illuminating as heaven or as shadowy as hell. A leader is a person who must take special responsibility for what's going on inside him or herself, inside his or her consciousness, lest the act of leadership create more harm than good.*[38]

This kind of admonishment is needed when attempting to address grassroots leadership, or any leadership. The fundamental principle here is that at all levels, and particularly at the grassroots level, the leader himself or herself must take time to do some inner work to understand, to reflect, and to go deeply enough so that the work inside will allow the work outside to be creative and fulfilling. The idea is that a spiritual journey within is one's gift to oneself.

Therefore, spiritual leadership is a major force for change within the grassroots leader and grassroots leadership. This, then, leads us to assumptions regarding the necessity and the desire for grassroots leadership to provide the necessary skills for African-American men and boys and their families to re-create their existence.

- Grassroots leadership can build community contacts by fostering programs that build capacity in communities. This can be stated in terms of the entire African-American Men and Boys initiative—some thirty programs—all of which are run by inspiring community leaders who are spiritually based and who exhibit moral leadership within their community.
- Grassroots leadership seeks to be engaged with a larger societal setting, as full participating citizens of not only the communi-

ty, but the society in general. The hallmark of a strong grass-roots democracy is that people are engaged in public, civic work.

- Grassroots leadership will engage all levels of society in a dialogue regarding the rights, responsibilities, and duties of all citizens within a democratic society.
- Grassroots leadership will provide a lens through which society can view this work at the community level for the first time, through the eyes of humane, moral leaders who are in touch with individuals—seeing the nature and the importance of this work as a way of reforming not only boys in trouble, but society at large.
- Grassroots leadership will be spiritually based, led by men and women who have made the voyage within as they create the platform upon which nationally shared values can be expressed. They are, in fact, "the restorers of streets."

RECOMMENDATIONS

The Task Force recommends that:

- Nationwide training be established for persons desiring to work as grassroots leaders in their communities, focusing on cultural and spiritual leadership.
- A two-year fellowship be created for men and women who wish to become grassroots leaders in their communities, with the object being to create grassroots democracy that would bring about a flourishing of their communities. These two-year fellowships would be funded on a competitive basis nationally and would work with combined funds of the nation's foundations.
- Local youth commissions be established within each community, run by grassroots civic leaders, with young people serving on those commissions to talk about their dreams and aspirations for themselves in their communities.

At the national level a commission of grassroots civic leaders be established to: (a) inventory current youth programs in the United States and abroad; (b) look at school-to-work models in other countries for possible use in this country; (c) develop a mechanism for early identification of young black male "diamonds in the rough" nationwide and match them with appropriate programs.

- The black middle class, along with the black church, explore various means of providing grassroots leaders and other community activists greater access to modern communication technology, particularly computers and related equipment.

• The idea of a learning plan be borrowed from the Kellogg National Fellowship Program, which would allow grassroots civic leaders to learn to develop year-to-year plans that would help to focus not only their work, but also teach African-American men and boys the skill of a yearly plan, to lay out simple, concrete steps to be followed to reach their particular dream. This learning plan would first establish their personal vision and then how they plan to attain that vision over the year. It would also have an all-encompassing vision as to what they would hope to accomplish in life and the steps that they would use to make this dream a reality.

Grassroots civic leaders could be instrumental in providing the hands-on daily work with these young men, helping them develop their learning plans and monitoring and advising them as these personal plans are developed. These plans could be a part of a journal process and could be expanded so that these boys could begin to find ways to create from chaos a controlled mechanism for planning their lives.

• Entrepreneurship be taught as early as first grade and continue to be taught throughout the educational process to familiarize African-American youth with business theory and practice.

• Foundations should act as capital providers for young beginning entrepreneurs.

• The National Foundation for Teaching Entrepreneurship to Handicapped and Disadvantaged Youths, and Cities and Schools are two programs that should be used because they provide youth with entrepreneurial training.

• A trust fund or venture capital fund should be established to provide capital for African-American males to purchase existing businesses.

• The black church and the black middle class must do more to promote business development within the local community. This includes establishing new business, establishing business partnerships with other community business groups, and providing financial and technical support for business development.

• A summit meeting should be held with the CEOs of the top two hundred (or more) corporations to discuss ways that these companies could provide financial and technical support for business development in local African-American communities.

• Michael Shuman's paper *Reclaiming the Inner City Through Political, Economic, and Ecological Self-Reliance* should be made the focus of a study group in order to explore how his ideas for local economic development might be implemented, through grassroots leaders.

- The church should provide forums for the community to discuss issues of local importance.
- A long-term workshop be created to combine resources and programs. Combined denominations should work together to bring new vitality to clergy.

7 CREATING COMMON GOOD: A New Democratic Process for Empowering the African-American Community

*H*OW can this idea of common good be manifested in the nation's urban centers, and how does the community create and meet common needs as a result? The recommendations in this chapter speak to entrepreneurship and economic development, educational reform, and commonwealth ideas.

Background

The fate of African-American men and boys is inextricably tied to creating the common good where their interests and values can be authentically connected to others, especially to the rest of America. Their survival is based on empowerment of the African-American community and the creation of vehicles that will allow them to express their deepest values and provide for their interests in the global world of economic and political competition. For our purposes in this report, we define the common good as set forth by Frances Moore Lappé in *Rediscovering America's Values*:

> *By common good I mean not what we as a people agree on in advance, but the good we seek in common through genuine dialogue. Its promise lies in the widely shared values of our diverse people, values that could form the basis of a renewed patriotism as love of country: pride in our society's fairness with opportunity for all. Pride in our commitment to promote life, so no one is denied the essentials*

93

*necessary to be a full member of society. Pride in safeguarding our
country's magnificent natural resources.*

*Further, unless we can conceive of ourselves as capable of consider-
ing the common good, it becomes utterly impossible to take into
account the interest of the yet-to-be born or the interest of nonhuman
life.*[39]

It is to this idea of common good that the Task Force was ultimately led in its discussion. The common good provided the means
to move to a discussion of the human condition.

The common good, of course, means more to members of this
Task Force than what government either does or does not do.
Essential to the common good is dialogue, as well as the development of good scholarship that illuminates the dark places. With dialogue and scholarship, three areas can receive attention that will
improve the common good: (1) a true reemphasis on entrepreneurship as a means of creating futures by creating wealth and having
each individual understand that he must become the center of his
own creative force; (2) the reform of education, so that it supports
entrepreneurship; and (3) technological development for African-
American men and boys.

These three issues are the springboard for establishing common
good within the African-American community struggling to be
reborn and to facilitate its connection to the larger community as
well.

Government and the Fracturing of Common Good

Many in the African-American community today do not perceive
government and the political process as a means of expressing their
values. This perception is not difficult to understand if one examines
the oppressive forces of government and a political system that has
been unresponsive to African-American interests and values. History
shows that government and the political system have their own self-
interests. As Jeremy Bentham noted in the Constitutional Code of
1830:

*Every body of men (including whatever body has the power to leg-
islate and to govern) is governed altogether by its conception of what
is its interest, in the narrowest and most selfish sense of the word
interest; never by a regard for the interest of the people.*

African-Americans can identify with Bentham's notion and realize that their hope for a common good rising above the melee of competing interests of government is dim, if not impossible. Government and the political system will, if left to their own devices, create their own agenda including the perpetuation of their own components of the bureaucracy. Thus, government and bureaucracy are not a force for good, particularly for African-Americans.

Public participation in the electoral process has been declining for decades. For eighteen- to twenty-four-year-olds, participation has historically been much lower than for the general population and has never topped 50 percent. Turnout of young African-Americans has been even more distressing. In 1992, only 31.9 percent of eligible eighteen- to twenty-four-year-old black men and 40.9 percent of young black women voted in the general elections as opposed to 43.3 percent of white men and 47.4 percent of white women in the same age group. Young black men are by far the most disaffected with regard to the political process. *Only 30 percent of the eighteen- to twenty-year-old black men are registered to vote*, and, of that number, *only 31.9 percent of them voted in the last election.*

It does appear at times that government and the economic system serve to encourage people to withdraw from acting independently. As Shuman noted in his paper titled "Reclaiming the Inner City Through Political, Economic, and Ecological Self-Reliance," there are several fundamental causes of disempowerment which must be addressed if the African-American community is to gain greater political and economic control of its daily life. These causes include:

- the growing public cynicism that government can do anything about it and wishful thinking that the "free market" can cure it;
- the feeling of being politically powerless and dropping out of the system;
- the fleeing of companies from the inner city to venues in the suburbs, the U.S.-Mexican border, and in the Third World;
- the lack of access to capital to invest in productive economic activity;
- the depletion of natural resources.[40]

Another example which might be cited by some African-Americans as a disengagement of the common good is the dismantling of affirmative action. Even though affirmative action did little to remove the legacy of racism in America or open doors fully to education and economic opportunities for the African-American community, it has served as a reminder to society that equity should be considered. America is not color blind, and the vestiges of discrimination permeate the education, economic, social, and political system.

However, there are many who felt that affirmative action was discriminatory, and even though it was enacted to reverse past practices of legal discrimination and segregation for over three hundred years, thirty years of affirmative action may be too much for the body politic of the nation to swallow. Consequently, the political climate in the country has moved to divest society of this particular instrument, which was instituted to bring about a level playing field for all Americans, particularly those who have been so harmed by the system over the past three hundred years.

A significant number of African-Americans continue to live in poverty. One out of three poor people living in the United States is African-American with over 1.2 million blacks living in "extreme poverty" neighborhoods in the one hundred largest cities, characterized by high levels of unemployment, poverty, drug addiction, violence, crime, and despair. This perilous condition is symbolized by:

- increasing incidence of homicide—which is the leading cause of death among black males fifteen to twenty-four years old;
- increasing number of murders, which occur every two hours;
- increasing incidence of suicide, which is committed every two days by a black boy under the age of twenty;
- increasing number of black boys being diagnosed with AIDS before their thirteenth birthday; and
- increasing number of black boys becoming victims of violent crimes—more than one in ten—134 of every 1,000 twelve- to fifteen-year-old black boys, and 147 of every 1,000 sixteen- to nineteen-year-old black males.

We cannot escape the reality that:

- there were 1,432 African-American inmates per 100,000 black U.S. residents in 1993 compared to only 203 per 100,000 for white Americans;
- over 300,000 black men are incarcerated, nearly 1,000 are on death row, and the median education level of those on death row is the tenth grade;
- every eleven minutes a black child is arrested for a violent crime;

- every four hours a black child dies from firearms; and
- one out of every four African-American children lives in a severely distressed neighborhood compared with one out of every sixty-three white children.

These disturbing figures threaten the ultimate destiny of black males, their families, and their community.

With the recent passage of the Crime Bill, the likelihood of getting an education while incarcerated has now been decimated. Pell grants to prisoners which provided inmates an opportunity to get an education, were eliminated. Thus, most if not all, correctional education programs have been forced to shut down. In addition, many prisoners who have begun educational programs to turn their lives around find themselves without classrooms. Now, the hope that these programs provided black males in prisons has been taken away.

The loss of educational opportunities while incarcerated contributes greatly to the problems that prisoners have in readjusting to the community when they are released. It is not difficult to see why they perceive the community as an enemy when they are placed in an environment that has become even more foreign to them. As a result of their incarceration, they now have a label which stymies acceptance. Moreover, they are reentering an environment that has been subject to many changes, especially in the job market where fundamental skills are required. The prisoner will be entering an environment where negative attitudes toward African-Americans still persist. All of these obstacles are real and have distinct implications for the future survival of African-Americans released from prison. In fostering a new democracy, African-Americans must find ways to reinstitute the provision of educational opportunities to black males during their tenure of incarceration.

Education Conditions

African-Americans have suffered in the worst way from the profound erosion of America's education system. The lack of discipline, decline of standards, inadequately trained teachers, insufficient local and state spending on education, and erosion of public support are some of the compelling problems facing American education, especially education in communities that serve black males. African-American boys are not being challenged and prepared with even the basic skills needed to compete successfully in the world of employment in an emerging global economy.

Since the early 1980s when America's public confidence in education reached an all-time high, the nation has launched a national framework for education reform. Federal legislation was enacted which stressed the need to make systemic changes to ensure equitable educational opportunities and high-level achievement for all students. Unfortunately, these education reform initiatives have had little, if any, impact on improving the educational conditions for African-American males. The schools attended by most continue to be plagued by lack of adequate funding, costly bureaucratic systems, poor educational facilities, lack of instructional equipment, and inadequately prepared teachers who are insensitive and incapable of effectively dealing with the education needs of black males. Such conditions, without question, have hampered the educational achievement of African-American males. They have reinforced the perception that America's education system continues to be unequal and incapable of serving all students.

The following statistics are a depressing profile of education for African-American males which substantiates the inequities in the system:

Nearly one out of every six black male students fourteen to nineteen years old is at least two grade levels behind;
African-American males in public schools are:
- 2.2 times as likely as white males to be placed in special education programs for mental retardation (one out of every thirty-four black male students are placed in such programs);
- 1.5 times as likely to be placed in programs for serious emotional disturbances (one out of every sixty-two black males);
- 2.7 times as likely to be corporally punished; and
Nearly one million students drop out of high school annually with a disproportionate number being young black men.

The dramatic demographic shifts in the traditional family structure have been identified as a serious issue in the African-American community that is affecting the education of youth. A growing number of families appear to be overwhelmed by the depth of their economic and social problems. With one or both parents in the work force, increasingly children are left unsupervised or older sisters and brothers are being forced to take on parenting responsibilities.

The Necessity for Good Parenting

Fundamentally, there is a lack of parenting in today's society. In the absence of fathers and parental guidance, drug dealers have become the caretakers of many young African-American men, providing them with easy access to the drug subculture. Unfortunately, in urban areas you will find that the drug pushers are spending more time with our young men than parents and educators. They seem to better know and understand the social demands and the ecology of African-American communities.

A rising demand is being felt for funds to support parenting initiatives: parenting clubs, organizations that would teach parenting skills, some formal way to help young men and women who are bringing children into the world to learn how to be parents under the conditions in which they live. This is an obvious and needed initiative that must be undertaken, not only by the nation's philanthropic organizations, but by the African-American civic, social, and religious organizations.

The lack of education among African-American parents is a major problem. Some parents are reading on the third or fourth grade level themselves, which raises serious questions as to how much they can help their children. However, many parents have not lost their enthusiasm, commitment, and dedication. They are genuinely concerned with the well-being of their children. They are willing to broaden their base of knowledge about parenting and how to play an effective role in educating their children.

Dr. Beverly Guy-Sheftall, a feminist scholar, spoke to the Task Force. Dr. Guy-Shetfall stressed the need to reevaluate the various issues which separate black men and women. Breaches between men and women lead to abuse, neglect, and gender-related issues such as homophobia, as well as the shocking attitude that black women are not capable of raising black boys. In her opinion, if we do not change this the African-American family and community are doomed.

Dr. Beverly Guy-Sheftall listed those things that she saw as important to creating a new sense of black male masculinity. She included:

a carefully constructed gender agenda encouraging dialogue and healing between men and women; new criteria for effective leadership in our community; open criticism of blatantly sexist individuals;

reclamation of our communities from a segment of the youth popula-
tion who have no intention of behaving in human ways; telling young
men that Frederick Douglass and W. E. B. DuBois fought for gender
equality. We need diverse voices and points of view surrounding the
important subject of black male identity formation.

She recommended that we search for strong male and female role models and treat them equally.

Boys, she stated, must be taught to respect the multiplicity of roles that men and women play. Also, mothers will have to learn to give their sons greater latitude in their role development.

The need for strong parenting programs for mothers and fathers is clearly a must for parents who find themselves in serious trouble with their offspring. But it is clearly necessary for any family where the burden of parenting is left to one spouse.

One of the most successful parenting programs to date is run by Charles Ballard. Ballard's program, the Institute for Responsible Fatherhood and Family Revitalization, located in Cleveland, Ohio, and Washington, D.C., is an exemplary model of what a grassroots organization can do to help parents, especially young men, assume their responsibility in the rearing of their children.

African-American children are coming to school both malnour- ished and unprepared for the demands of a competitive academic environment. Consideration should be given to investing in African- American children before they are born through *parental education* designed to promote healthy lifestyles and healthy nutritional prac- tices.

We saw the collapse of a common-good issue when national health care failed to win support. It is obvious that this issue of national health care is a primary one if we are to talk about what we hold in common and what we would like to see all Americans have if they are to be healthy and able to participate and work in this society. It would appear that we have not had the appropriate dia- logue to bring together the common-good ideas from all sides of the political, social, and economic spectrum in order to bring this about. There is a gaping hole in the human condition of this society if it cannot, in some way, come to grips with and understand that all American citizens must have adequate health-care coverage.

More important than that, and what might lead this dialogue, is to talk about how to prevent health care problems from occurring in the first place. Therefore, discussion on the prevention of health problems and a look at alternative medicine related to mind and body should be undertaken. This may be one of the most important common good dialogue issues that this nation could undertake. It cuts across all class, color, and gender lines, and it could provide the very essence of community building and grassroots leadership—prevention of illness and creation of sound mind-body relationships.

For a very long time health professionals have made it a point to say that violence is a public health issue. And while we agree with them that violence is a public health issue, we also restate the fact that violence is merely a symptom. A comprehensive national conversation on public health policies, public health coverage, and preventive formulas for keeping all Americans morally, spiritually, and physically healthy, is necessary for building our national common good.

Violence

A definite threat to African-American males in schools is the alarming increase of violence. Children are dying at a rate of one every two hours, 25 every two days in gun violence. Between 1970 and 1991, about 50,000 children were killed by guns. This year, we will lose 5,000 more. The sad commentary about these statistics is that a great deal of the violence is taking place in schools and the record number of children killing children grows larger.

In educating African-American males for the 21st century, it is crucial to reshape their aspirations. We need to show them more positive outcomes by:

- developing long-term efforts for linking early education to entrepreneurship and successful entry into the economic complex of American life;
- using internships provided by the private sector to bridge school to work;
- creating rewards for achievement in school;
- exposing students to positive role models;
- exposing students to entrepreneurship as part of their career awareness in elementary school;
- developing "Junior Achievement" (business orientation programs) in elementary school;
- providing mentoring programs at all levels of the education continuum;

- developing community-based education programs in the African-American neighborhoods.

Schools need to place greater emphasis on building partnerships in the community to make after-school time educationally productive for children. Research on education reform tells us that children spend only 9 percent of the calendar year in school. In view of this limited amount of children's time spent in school, it is imperative that increased attention be paid to learning outside of the classroom environment.

The Task Force believes it is now time to look at school as a day-long process, beginning at 7:30 or 8:00 A.M., and ending at 6:00 P.M. This would provide a major boost to parents who are working. It would provide for safe streets, and it would allow children longer to focus on what their lives will be like. It is obvious that some kind of task force would have to be developed to determine what this day-long school would look like, as well as how it would be staffed and operated. Community people might be used in some portion of the day to do actual formal teaching, especially the values, ethics, and duties that members of the community polis would hold.

The task force would also look at school as a year-round phenomenon, as opposed to a nine-month one.

Social/Economic Conditions

There seems to be growing agreement that of the many problems facing the nation today, none looms larger than the social and economic condition of an increasing number of African-American men and boys. The shift from manufacturing to an information and service economy, compounded by the absence of sustained federal and private investment in the well-being of those crippled by poverty and social alienation, has created structural impediments in the economy that are insurmountable for those who lack the education or skills to compete in a borderless marketplace that has no nationality and no national allegiance.

It is beyond dispute that "Dollars, despite the patriotic slogans on the bills, have no nationality. . . . Globalization of the marketplace transcends the national interest, outlook and strategy."[41]

The social and economic barriers facing African-American men and boys are further exacerbated by the absence of national development initiatives on a global scale and the growing mismatch between the demands of the marketplace and the skills and educational level of African-American men and boys.

In the midst of worldwide redistribution of economic power, downsizing, reengineering, and reinventing government and corporate America, those who lack "value added" competencies and highly technical skills are deemed dispensable as measured by their inability to produce wealth. "As the world of work turns ever faster on its computer-imaged, digitally controlled, micro-processed axis, companies increasingly need a scientific and technically competent work force," as stated in a recent article on integrating the world enterprise. Indeed, the United States is no longer the economic engine of the world. Moreover, Americans are no longer under the illusion that government can create permanent job and psychic security.

Globalization of the United States economy has contributed to the absence of national investment in the nation's urban cities, undermining the ability of local communities to create avenues toward self-sufficiency, disrupting domestic policies and practices traditionally fostered by national and state governments. "Thus, in the fulfillment of its global vision, both justice and stability are eluded."[42] Within this decade, the federal investment in improving the quality of life in the black communities of America declined from 11.5 percent to 3.8 percent, seriously undercutting the ability to restore communities with large concentrations of poor and neglected populations. As highlighted in *Three Realities: Minority Life in the U.S.*, "by virtually all statistical indicators of income, opportunity, education, access to health care, and personal security, it is clear that the typical minority American does not begin to enjoy anything close to parity with the life experiences of the average white American."[43] Yet, by the year 2000, minorities will account for 60 percent of the total population growth in the nation and the black population will total 35 million, an increase of 16 percent compared with 7 percent for white Americans.

In a profit-driven society, African-American men and boys are engaged in their own demise, leaving their families and communities abandoned in an urban conclave of poverty surrounded by suburban prosperity. Today, white families have ten times the median wealth of black families. The median net worth in 1992 for black households with monthly incomes of $3,884 and above was $47,160, for whites it was $119,000. Further, census reports note that 10 percent of the population controls nearly 80 percent of all the nation's wealth. When confronted with overwhelming evidence that African-

American men and boys are facing catastrophic economic challenges, the nation continues to foster old social policies that have failed miserably.

The nation's ambivalence toward the human condition of African-American men and boys contributes to the intractability of inequality and essentially reinforces barriers in the economy inhibiting educational, social, and economic parity. More than any other American racial and ethnic group, the future of African-American men and boys is acutely threatened by:

- displacement of industry and the absence of an economic base in poor communities;
- low educational achievement and the lack of value-added skills.
- inadequate nutrition, housing, and health;
- destabilization of the African-American family structure;
- prevalence of crime, violence, and institutionalization;
- chronic unemployment and underemployment;
- failure to be engaged in civic life and responsibilities.

National social policies and programs deeply embedded in the culture of government and the private sector reinforce structural barriers in the economy that foster privilege and power for white males at the expense of a growing population of African-American men and boys isolated from the mainstream of American society. In an increasingly competitive and socially stratified society, African-American men are left with few if any political options and even fewer social options that offer concrete solutions for creating legitimate and self-sufficient economic alternatives.

The flight of industries from urban to rural communities is supported by government and political systems because of their own self-interests. Using the theme that the key to a national well-being is to offer the world's corporations the best-educated work force and most efficient infrastructure for transportation and communication, the national government feels it should pick the winners and losers among communities. Needless to say, African-Americans must question the common good when government and politicians stress that it is better to move unemployed workers to the most attractive and competitive communities than to move investment and jobs to communities with the highest level of unemployment.

Economic empowerment of the African-American community must be realized if America is to maintain its dominant and leadership role as a major industrial nation. The country cannot afford, in a rapidly changing global marketplace, not to build a highly skilled and knowledgeable work force. The nation will have to make an investment—an investment in equality of opportunity that is far beyond what has been done to date.

In looking to the future and potential opportunities that will contribute to the economic empowerment of African-American men and boys, attention must be given to the federal government's initiatives in the development of empowerment or enterprise zones, the increasing sensitivity of corporations about their commitment to the community in which they are located, and the millions of dollars many corporations are spending on retraining. Attention must also be directed to making connections with small businesses and increasing the pressure on Congressional leaders and policy makers to abolish the discrimination that has prevented the building of a highly skilled and knowledgeable African-American work force.

It is difficult to discuss the economic conditions of African-American men and boys without referring to entrepreneurism. Despite the progress that has been made over the past two decades, the lack of achievement in this area further exacerbates the economic condition of the African-American family. The barriers to African-American entrepreneurism include:

- the lack of African-Americans as merchants, shop owners, service providers;
- the absence of ongoing training efforts within the community to establish a base of entrepreneurs;
- the operation of businesses within the community by "outsiders" who do not hire or train community members;
- the lack of incentives to incorporate the community;
- the absence of role models—entrepreneurs from within the community—who provide young African-Americans with positive images to emulate;
- the breakdown of the education process between elementary and high school years, which disrupts the flow of the resources needed to create a merchant class within the community;
- the absence of capital in the community, which does not allow for investment possibilities.

Parallel Economies

Parallel economies would provide the best opportunity for African-Americans in America's urban ghettos to become entrepreneurs on the scale in which they can participate, invest, and grow. They cannot jump from urban poverty into the global economy. This parallel economy, as framed and developed by Michael Shuman in conjunction with Bobby Austin's concept of a parallel economy for low-income areas, could be a workable new economic system. The following excerpt is taken from Shuman's paper:

> *A creative approach to developing inner cities is to delink their economies from the national and global economy and to increase their level of self-reliance. This approach is at odds with neoliberal trade theory, which postulates that global free trade, open markets, and economic transactions unrelated to place are in everyone's interests. Even the seminal architect of trade theory, David Ricardo, however, understood that in a world of free trade there would be winners and losers. Only if some of the gains were redistributed from the winners to the losers could everyone benefit from the trade.*
>
> *In point of fact, redistribution in the United States over the past century has hardly occurred at all.[44] Indeed, throughout the 1980s income and wealth were redistributed from the poor to the rich. The lowest income group received less income over this period (dropping from 5.6 to 4.6 percent of all income), while the highest income group received more (from 40.6 to 44.0 percent).[45] Between 1979 and 1989, the top 1 percent of all earners saw their incomes double.[46] The regressive distribution is even more dramatic with respect to wealth. The richest 1 percent of Americans expanded their wealth holdings between 1983 and 1992 from 31 to 37 percent.[47] That 1 percent now holds as much wealth as the poorest 40 percent of the American people.*
>
> *In the absence of real redistribution, the inner cities that are the clear losers in the mainstream economy certainly can justify withdrawing from it. There are, of course, legal limits to how far a community can go in delinking (the Commerce Clause of the Constitution, for example, prohibits local tariffs), and it is easy to dismiss the principle of self-reliance by pointing to many complex products that communities cannot manufacture on their own. The real goal of self-reliance, however, is much more modest: A community should seek to increase control over its own economy as far as practicable within the bounds of the law. Residents of a community should seek to maximize local investment in local businesses, local consump-*

tion of locally manufactured goods or locally provided services, and local hiring of local workers. This way, dollars can circulate repeatedly within the community and ensure greater levels of employment, business, income, and wealth for everyone living there.

Local Reinvestment

Even communities with high levels of poverty have substantial stores of wealth in the form of checking and savings accounts, pension funds, stocks and bonds, and surplus municipal revenues. Typically, residents, city workers, and municipal officials invest these monies in institutions located outside the community or in securities or mutual funds unconnected to the community. Billions of dollars leak out of the inner city and never come back.

Credit is important for several reasons.[48] Without establishing a history of borrowing and repayment, low-income earners can never qualify for major loans for housing or business. A neighborhood made up primarily of renters rather than owners remains transient and allows rental incomes to go to landlords who live outside the community. If owners or renters are unable to obtain repair loans, the quality of the housing deteriorates and the riskiness—and interest rates—of loans increases. As long as business loans are unaffordable or unavailable, residents must go to work for entrepreneurs elsewhere and the local economy remains stagnant. As James Head and Kelly Mogul argue, "In modern American society, access to credit is one of the few routes to economic progress for those who are not born into privilege."[49]

How can credit be made increasingly available to the inner city? One available tool is the Community Reinvestment Act (CRA), enacted originally in 1977 and amended several times since.[50] The main purpose of the CRA was to outlaw lending discrimination and the "redlining" of poor neighborhoods as bad credit risks. But it also places affirmative obligations on banks and financial institutions receiving federal insurance to invest some of their capital in the community, particularly in low- and moderate-income areas.[51] Federal authorities enforce the Act by requiring banks to release information about their lending patterns and by evaluating how well they are reinvesting in the community. The Association of Community Organizations for Reform Now (ACORN) and other organizations have been able to use the CRA to pressure banks (through adverse publicity, protests, and boycotts) to behave more responsibly, but the Act's criteria for community-friendly performance are loose and enforcement is lax. Many loans that federal regulators deem beneficial to the community, for example, in fact benefit primarily local developers or government pet projects (like stadiums or conference centers) that contribute little to the economic well-being of people living under the poverty line.

There are other kinds of initiatives state and local governments could take to press banks to improve the quantity and quality of local reinvestment. Public pension funds or surplus municipal monies might be invested only in banks prioritizing progressive community reinvestment. Linda Tarr-Whelan, director of the Center for Policy Priorities, estimates that "if state public employee pension systems alone invested just 2 percent of their portfolios in economically targeted investments, this would yield $100 billion dollars worth of investment capital to create jobs and growth in our capital-starved neighborhoods."[52] State and local governments also might support such banks with public contracts, tax breaks, and zoning variances.

A bolder approach might be for a state or city to use public funds to start its own anti poverty bank. An important lesson in the value of credit can be learned from Bangladesh, where for over a decade the Grameen Bank has been giving small loans (roughly $50) to poor women to start their own businesses. Women are favored because they are seen as handling money more responsibly than men, who often waste their paycheck on liquor and gambling. The bank gives loans to women organized in five-person collectives, who support each other in the design and execution of their business plans. Once one person in the collective successfully repays the first $50 loan, a second loan is given to the second person in the collective, and so forth. The Grameen Bank not only provides loans but also trains recipients in the basics of running a business. The bank has achieved a repayment rate of 97 percent, remarkable even by Western standards.

America's inner cities should explore setting up their own Grameen Banks. To a limited extent, this has already happened through several private initiatives. The South Shore Bank in Chicago provides small-scale loans to refurbish low-income housing. The Good Faith Fund gives modest loans to start-up businesses in rural Arkansas. The Community Capital Bank specializes in loans for small businesses, not-for-profits, and affordable multi-unit housing in low income and moderate income areas of New York City. But these programs, while commendable, do not incorporate all the innovations of Grameen. They do not focus exclusively on the poor (sometimes the recipients are middle class), they do not target women, they do not set up support groups, and they usually do not provide much in the way of business training.

One noteworthy program that does focus on women and rely on support groups is Working Capital, a nonprofit program based in Cambridge, Massachussetts.[53] Since 1991, it has provided more than 1,300 loans worth more than a million dollars to 770 small business owners. First-time loan recipients get $500, and once a repayment record is established, new loans are issued in successively larger sizes, up to $5,000. Working Capital obtains loan capital from regional and local banks, foundations, corporations, and federal agencies. Its repayment rate is 98 percent.

New efforts, more systematically following the design of Grameen but tailored to the needs of people living in America's inner cities, are necessary. These could be privately owned and run, or if private investors cannot be found, a local government might own and run the bank. Securities laws need to be changed so that deposits in these institutions can be federally insured. Individuals and institutions (like foundations) could be encouraged to use these institutions as savings banks. Employees and labor unions could press their pension fund managers to invest in such banks.

President Bill Clinton was taken with the idea of community banking during the 1992 campaign and promised to spend a billion dollars to set up 100 community development banks like the South Shore Bank of Chicago.[54] Mainstream banks, however, also wanted to be eligible for government subsidies and conditioned their support of Clinton's proposal on the loosening of federal oversight of banks. The final law on "Community Development Financial Institutions," passed in 1994, offers limited matching support for both for-profit and not-for-profit financial institutions.[55] The billion dollars initially proposed was pared down to $382 million. As one advocate of community lending noted, the bill is "just a beginning when you compare it to the need for affordable credit. It's just a small down payment."[56]

States and cities also might press the largest pension fund in the world to invest in antipoverty banks—that is, the U.S. Social Security System. In theory, monies given to Social Security are held in trust until a person reaches retirement (or becomes blind or disabled), and in the interim these trust funds are to be reinvested. In fact, over 90 percent of the surplus funds in Social Security are being invested in nonmarketable Treasury notes to reduce the federal deficit.[57] If the deficit gradually gets repaid, more Social Security funds will be available for reinvestment, potentially in urban anti-poverty projects. The total size of the Social Security Trust fund was $330 billion in 1992, and is expected to grow to $4.2 trillion over the next twenty-five years.[58]

Another potential source of funding for antipoverty banks is the Federal Reserve Bank. Economist Norman Kurland has suggested that the Fed establish a two-tiered interest structure: higher interest for credit for consumption and lower interest for credit for productive investment.[59] Using the lower rate, the Fed could enact an "Industrial Homestead Act," which would help provide credit to individuals, employees, or communities that needed low-interest credit to invest in business ventures. The charter of the Fed, which has always embraced the goal of full employment, could be revised to focus increases in national credit on productive, antipoverty loans.

Local Purchasing

Local purchasing is perhaps even more important in the inner city than local reinvestment, because the poor must spend most of their income, not on investing, but on consuming basic goods such as food, housing, utilities, and health care. Whenever a citizen buys a good made locally or uses a local service, he or she protects local jobs, strengthens the local economy, and enlarges the local tax base. Every dollar spent on locally produced goods provides income to local owners, local workers, and local suppliers. If they, in turn, spend their income on locally produced goods, the local economic multiplier continues to pump the community economy.

Local Hiring

The virtues of hiring local residents for local jobs are obvious: more employment in the community, more spending, more tax revenues, and less crime. The previous section suggested some of the ways a *community could expand employment, particularly for low-skill, low-wage workers. But employment policies should be equally concerned with retaining high-skill, high-wage workers within the community.*

Policy makers today are at loggerheads over various proposals to help African-Americans. Should welfare be expanded, transformed, or eliminated? What qualifies or disqualifies a poor person as "deserving" of government assistance? Should income assistance be given in universal or targeted programs? Should affirmative action be pushed or abolished? These questions, however, while important, are beside the point.

If poverty-stricken African-Americans live disproportionately in inner cities, and if urban poverty is disproportionately black, then the most crucial question is quite different: How can we transform America's ghettos from crucibles of despair into thriving communities of hope? If the analysis of this report is correct, the crucial answers relate not to welfare or affirmative action, but to new strategies for community development. And to accomplish this, communities need to go beyond the conventional nostrums about job training or attracting private enterprise.

If there is any lesson for America's ghettos to learn from history, it is that they must take care of themselves, because no one else will. The local governments overseeing economically stagnant neighborhoods must seek to expand their political power, to revitalize local politics, and to secure jobs through checks and balances on mobile corporations. If an insufficient number of private businesses are willing to rise responsibly to the local economic challenge, the community must be willing to open its own factories, banks, and WPA-style programs. These public responses may even be preferable to private ones, because ultimately they leave the community with greater power over its own destiny. Such power will be essential if communities are to realize the potential benefits from local investment, local purchasing, local hiring, and local resource self-sufficiency.

Even if the main focus of creative policy making should be local, there are many supportive policies that are needed at higher levels of governance. The states must give communities more power to tax, spend, regulate, borrow, and take economic initiative. The federal government must enact campaign finance reform, narrow the grounds for federal preemption of local law, and provide federal insurance and

more credit from the Fed to antipoverty banks. And rules of GATT
and free trade need to be fundamentally rethought, with the interests
of community self-reliance in mind.

Ultimately, however, the most important catalyst for enacting these
policies is a lively, engaged civil society. Harvard political scientist
Robert Putnam recently examined the performance of 20 regional
governments in Italy. The administrations he found that were most
successful at "creating innovative day care programs and job-training
centers, promoting investment and economic development, pioneering
environmental standards and family clinics" also had the highest lev-
els of civic engagement.[60] Key indicators of civic engagement were
"voter turnout, newspaper readership, membership in choral societies
and literacy circles, Lions Clubs, and soccer clubs." Social networks
provided for "organized reciprocity and civic solidarity" and included
"guilds, religious fraternities, cooperatives, mutual aid societies,
neighborhood associations,"[61]

These communities did not become civic simply because they were
rich. The historical record strongly suggests precisely the opposite: they
have become rich because they were civic. The social capital embodied
in norms and networks of civic engagement seems to be a precondi-
tion for economic development, as well as for effective government.
Development economists take note: civics matter.[62]

Putnam's findings suggest that the conclusions of Nichols Lemann,
Robert Reich, and others, that we should abandon America's worst-off
communities, are dead wrong. Within these communities are vital
untapped reservoirs of personal commitment, cultural heritage, reli-
gious tradition, social solidarity, economic power, and political
willpower. There are millions of people who, with proper organizing,
empowerment, credit, and supportive public policy, are prepared to
dedicate their lives to bettering their communities. Rather than aban-
don America's inner cities because of the assets they lack, we should
nurture the assets they have.[63]

The main objective of one or more parallel economies is to
intentionally create small-scale economic systems within urban
areas that are maintained by investors in those areas, an infrastructure that could be supported by technology, cottage industry, "Mom-
and-Pop" stores, open markets, crafts, etc. that would be located
within a community or accessible through the World Wide Web. The

capital to create them could be from any source and training could be conducted through the proposed "Technology Centers" in the various communities.

Technology

American society is being primed for greater reliance on technology, which has enormous implications for African-Americans who must find a way to participate in technology-based activities. Technology has unlimited capacity for education, social, economic, and personal development. It offers African-American men and boys the best opportunity to escape the baggage put upon them by society at large of being violent, uncreative, unmotivated, or ineducable. Mastery of the brave new world of technology offers an independent foundation from which to move the world. Through its instant global access, it allows the user to have his ideas seen and assessed without the necessity of personal contact.

A matter not often discussed when talking about education is the disproportionate number of African-American children being placed in special-education programs. A substantial number of black males are being diagnosed as behaviorally disordered—a disability which is perceived to be catastrophic, incurable, and a prelude to criminal acts and incarceration. African-American boys are being diagnosed by individuals who have no credentials in psychological assessment and whose standards or criteria for their diagnosis are based on the negative attitudes perpetuated in society about black males. This nefarious labeling has detrimental consequences for African-American males, making it difficult for them to get a quality education and develop the essential skills for future employment.

In the continuing quest for education reform, schools need to increase their use of technology. Technology can be an excellent resource for streamlining school administrative functions and a powerful tool in the instructional arena. Student learning can be appreciably enhanced through the use of technological tools. In particular, they can be used to equip students with the skills they need to seek future employment.

One of the more fundamental new community institutions is the "Technology Center." Technology centers must become the new youth centers in America's urban areas. African-American men and boys would be attracted, from what we can determine, to these centers. These technology centers could act as magnets for the development of skills that these boys possess in hand and eye coordination. Technology centers could be a way of creating a whole new world out of which these boys could make some sense of what their futures could be like. These technology centers would be established in community institutions, churches, lodges, wherever people wished to have them. They should be developed in such a way as to have linkages with private industry around the world.

These technology centers would help to create a particular kind of new commonwealth experience, because they would hold in common with the rest of the nation that which is becoming commonplace—the use of the personal computer—not only for communication, but for job development, and for information. Without these capabilities, grassroots democracy cannot take hold in these communities, because they will have no way to communicate with the outside world as they attempt to fulfill their own dreams and to align with the rest of American society.

By the turn of the twenty-first century, it is estimated that 70 percent of all jobs will be computer related, and those who are computer illiterate will average only three-quarters the salary of others. Based on these statistics, a vastly reduced quality of life awaits the "know-nots" of the future. African-Americans, therefore, must inform themselves of the enormous empowerment potential that computer-enhanced technology represents.

Universities and colleges should mobilize the African-American community in order to assist them in becoming technology competent. They need to show the community how to use technology in addressing social problems and particularly in the education of African-American males. Technological tools have unlimited capacity for presenting academic matters to individuals, effecting better communication, and individualizing instruction.

Scholarship

The human condition, as conceived of by the Task Force, and as it relates to civil life for African-American men and boys, cannot be fully examined without reevaluating arts and letters in American society. America's distortion of history, creating the myth of black inferiority and white superiority, continues to have a devastating impact on African-American men and boys. Academic institutions must address these distortions in a manner that moves the nation toward understanding that all members of the society are contributing to that society, and that is what makes America great.

One of the most important ways in which African-American scholars can play a key role in the education of young students is to ensure that appropriate attention is directed toward strong academic programs focusing on science, math, and computer sciences. Substantial evidence exists which shows a high correlation between students' self-concept and educational achievement. It is important for students to feel that they are of worth to the society in which they live. African-American scholars and academic institutions have a responsibility to assist students in developing a positive self-concept. Students need to hear what scholars have learned from the lessons of life and know that they are not alone.

There is an abundance of research which shows that if students are treated as bright, loving, and talented individuals, they will live up to those expectations and more than likely become that type of person. Thus, it is important that African-American scholars manifest and model the kind of behavior that they wish to see youth learn. Youth tend not to question scholars' expectations, they only live up to what is expected of them. They respond to successful role models that will connect them to the larger African-American community.

Historically black colleges and universities must exercise a stronger leadership role in recruiting and retaining students, especially at the graduate level. They need to instill in these students the requisite research skills for producing scholarly work that will empower the African-American community. These students need role models. This suggests that African-Americans holding doctorates should spend part of their career in higher education in a historically black college or university. This would provide a unique opportunity for them to advance scholarship, serve as a role model, and mentor students.

Building Grassroots Democracy

There is an increasing commitment of African-Americans to reclaim their community out of which will emerge a common good. This is supported by Haki Madhubuti, who, in his recent book, *Claiming Earth*, stresses that African-Americans must articulate a politic of empowerment at both an individual and community level that is intimately tied to education, economics, social and environmental development, and human politics for the many, rather than the few.

During the past three decades, African-Americans have created many organizations and have provided leadership in many initiatives designed to advance the cause of black Americans. Some have failed and some have been successful. Most important at this time in our history, African-Americans need to take what has been learned and use it to engage the wider society as that society attempts to help to build a new, grassroots democratic process. In particular, we need to take the successes, which are fragmented, and connect them to create the necessary power base for change. The successes can be used to build relationships, confront conditions which have deprived African-Americans of true participation in American society, and contribute to the building of a new community polis.

The time has arrived for African-Americans, especially black males, to move from victimhood to self-reliance, to ownership of self, of resources, and of their future. They must conceive of themselves as capable of creating common good. The African-American community must make an investment. The community must come together and unite its efforts to improve the quality of life for African-American men and boys. A new dialogue must take place. Other Americans must be challenged to connect with the interests of the African-American community and participate in creating a space wherein an equitable and inclusive common good is constructed.

The structural impediments that have constricted educational, social, and economic opportunities for African-American men and boys will have to be challenged more aggressively than they have in the past. The challenge of removing structural barriers is systemic and, thus, the creating of social, educational, and economic opportunities for African-American men and boys must also be systemic. While more national policies and programs are needed to stimulate public and private investment in severely depressed communities, there must be a radical change in the quality of public education for African-American children, families, and particularly men and boys.

In communities throughout the country there are many exemplary initiatives which address the barriers to education, social, economic, and individual development of African-American men and boys. These successful initiatives are making a profound difference in the lives of black males. They are providing a new sense of hope, an inspiration, an opportunity to build one's own capacity, and an opportunity to build new partnerships. Without question, these initiatives offer much for empowering the African-American community, but widespread knowledge about their existence and attributes is absent. They are virtually invisible, which is the very reason that, as part of the strategy for building a new democracy in the African-

American community, emphasis must be placed on developing ways for disseminating information about exemplary programs and advancing opportunities for replication.

A dialogue must take place that explores the human condition and builds a new consensus for change among African-Americans. This dialogue must be built on a foundation of hope—hope for creating a common good and increasing prosperity among African-Americans. The agenda calls for America to alter the structural impediments that have negated the educational, economic, and social empowerment of the African-American community. It challenges Americans to connect with the interests of African-Americans and build a system that is equitable and inclusive in raising the competitiveness of the nation. The agenda challenges America, from a community democracy point of view, to create a common good out of which will emerge the advancement of opportunities for the African-American community.

A National Community Youth Policy

There is not a coordinated approach to the general welfare of African-American boys. The Task Force believes that a national youth policy should be developed that would encourage a partnership between families, educational institutions, religious institutions, foundations, business, and government. This policy would make such partnership its base. The policy would be the driving force behind the Task Force's Integrated Action Plan.

RECOMMENDATIONS

The Task Force recommends that:

- A philanthropic organization be created that will address the plight of black males and proclaim the contributions that they have made to American society. This proposed organization would orchestrate a crusade for building a new consensus among African-Americans and attempt to successfully deal with government to stimulate systemic change relative to African-American men and boys. The organization would continue the dialogue initiated by the National Task Force on African-American Men and Boys aimed at creating a new community democracy, one that will authentically empower the black community, foster a new consensus, and empower individuals to become leaders.
- The proposed philanthropic organization or National Foundation be charged with creating a National Task Force on the "Education and

Economic Empowerment of the African-American Community." This task force would identify successful education and economic empowerment programs, organize community dialogues using the focus group concept and latest technological tools, devise new strategies that would be effective in restructuring the American education system for improved educational outcomes, and reengineering the workplace for increasing employment and greater participation of African-Americans in the economy. The task force would also sponsor a summit meeting designed to develop strategies for confronting the issues negating the education and economic empowerment of the African-American community.

• The proposed task force should be charged with the creation of five centers of excellence strategically located in different areas of the country to serve as catalysts for stimulating change in the education and employment systems. These centers would serve as the central community agencies to assist in developing collaborative efforts for building a community democracy, advancing the education and employment of youth, providing supplemental instruction resources for African-American youth, making available a resource and conversation/dialogue arena for parents and other stakeholders in the community concerned with education and employment, organizing a clearinghouse for the dissemination of information on successful program initiatives, and training in democratic effectiveness. The centers would also provide training in technology, including the design, management, and replication of products and programs that will prepare participants for the workplace of the twenty-first century. The programs in technology would introduce new teaching materials and software suitable for confidence building, skills development, and employment readiness of African-American young men and boys. The programs would also work with existing information sources and create new materials as necessary to package multimedia courseware appropriate to distance learning delivered through a variety of telecommunications technologies as well as through a variety of public and private organizational vehicles. (An ideal resource for the establishment of the five centers of excellence is the available military bases that are being closed throughout the country. Facilities, equipment, and other educational resources exist for utilization. Moreover, there is the potential engagement of military personnel in teaching and participation in the education and economic empowerment of the African-American community. This investment by government would yield exceptional benefits for the welfare of society.) Like the charter school concept, the proposed centers of excellence could become one of the most unique educational enterprises by the turn of the century.

• The proposed task force should develop a plan for creating and instituting a year-round school program. As mentioned earlier, children only spend 9 percent of the calendar year in school. Coupled with this is the fact that the school environment consumes only six hours of a child's day, leaving eighteen hours each weekday plus the hours on weekends and holidays available for other activities. We need to extend the school year as well as provide additional pathways to academic achievement. Use of this additional time could be invaluable for improving the quality of education, especially for African-American youth.

• The proposed task force should develop a plan for expanding the residential school concept for young African-American males. The task force would study the five established boarding schools and extract ideas for expanding the enrollment at those schools as well as pursue the development of regionally accessible boarding schools for boys who need to be removed from their present environment. A principal at an inner-city school in Washington, D.C., recently proposed that the school be used as a residential facility on weekends for African-American youth who need to be removed from their present environment. A special area of the school would be utilized for sleeping accommodations and an enrichment program would be offered to involve the youth in constructive academic activities. Parents, community leaders, and teachers would work collaboratively in providing the youth academic information, character-building experiences, and organized recreational activities. Such a program would provide an ideal opportunity to expose the youth to technology and build their skills in the use of computers, which would have significant implications for their future.

• The proposed task force should orchestrate the development and implementation of a series of civic forums via interactive teleconferencing. The forums, which would have as their overarching theme "Extending the Family: Taking Charge," would provide a continuing dialogue on the themes identified by the National Task Force on African-American Men and Boys. The forums would also be used to encourage the participation of the various black professional associations in the dialogue.

• The proposed task force should re-create the Black Academy of Arts and Letters. The purpose of the Academy would be to assemble a group of outstanding African-American scholars who would develop and implement strategies for enhancing black scholarship. Other functions of the Academy would include building connections between academic institutions and their community, recruiting students for careers as scholars, and increasing the matriculation of African-American males in colleges and universities.

• The proposed task force should establish George Washington Carver Clubs throughout the United States for young African-Americans to be involved in the process of inventing and entrepreneurship. The purpose of these clubs would be to form the basis of technology centers with all of the necessary technological and scientific equipment to provide youth the beginning step toward inventing new and better futures. They would be developed in communities, churches, and youth centers and implemented by teachers and other activists in the technology field.

• The proposed task force should confront schools with respect to changing the academic curriculum to include the teaching of entrepreneurship in the first grade and throughout the grade-school years. Schools should teach children what business is and how it operates. African-American children, in particular, need to be taught about the American economy and how it works. They need to be taught how to participate in the economic development of the country. Schools must restructure their curriculum to integrate information on entrepreneurship and use entrepreneurship programs that will provide limited exposure for students. The programs should provide several components which include real-world relevance; a learning-by-doing component; activities that are entrepreneurial; activities that provide incentives early on that are built into the model; and activities that provide for the development of strong dedicated leadership.

• A summit on "Images of African-American Men and Boys" should be held to develop and implement strategic initiatives for portraying a more positive image of African-American men and boys. The purpose of the summit would be to assemble the CEOs of the nation's major media outlets (television, newspapers, radio) and key newscasters to increase their understanding of the plight of African-American men and boys, and how the media can change the portrayal of violence and other factors which provide the basis for forming negative opinions of black males. The Corporation for Public Broadcasting might be asked to host the proposed summit meeting.

• A summit meeting of at least two hundred CEOs of the top corporations should be held to develop a business plan and strategies for encouraging the development of entrepreneurship opportunities among African-American males. The summit would identify foundations and corporations who could act as capital providers for young beginning entrepreneurs, create a small venture capital fund and policies and procedures for accessing such a fund, and examine the potential purchase of established operating businesses that would provide greater possibilities for entrepreneurs to succeed.

• A Technology Center Study Group should be established. This study group would be charged with developing the prototype for an extended school day after-school program, focusing on science, math, computer science, and entrepreneurship; and would be a joint venture between private industry, the community, and possibly the educational system. This program would work year-round, and it would bring to bear upon boys throughout these communities the very best in computer services so that they can become proficient in the creation of new knowledge.

8 RESTORING COMMUNITY

*T*HE Task Force Subcommittee on Housing and Community Development was charged with the task of identifying strategies and tactics for the restoration of weakened communities. Beset by chronic unemployment, poverty, crime and violence associated with the drug trade, and a lack of social and often municipal services, these weakened communities are the major source of troubled African-American men and boys. No one doubts that a causal relationship exists. Individual behavior is influenced and reinforced by community and environment. As distressed communities are improved, so are the lives and life choices of their residents. The restoration of communities results in restored hope for people.

Background

A good community, at its core, is a place of peace and safety that provides opportunity for full human development. The well-being of a community is the sum of its physical, economic, and social natures. It is easy to see a community as a place: homes, schools, streets, parks, churches, shops. These make up the physical infrastructure of community; their soundness and attractiveness is essential for a good community. Community also includes economic infrastructure: jobs, businesses, education, sources of capital and investment. Without economic life and opportunity, a community cannot meet its material needs and a good quality of life cannot be enjoyed. Most importantly, perhaps, community is a social and political organization which embodies elements necessary for getting (or keeping) its physical and economic life. These less tangible elements make up a social infrastructure which creates the polis, a place where people strive to meet their needs, have cultural and historic bonds, and which is characterized by a sense of community. Social infrastructure is built on public kinship and civic storytelling, which give people a place in their society; and on an understanding of a common good expressed through a civic and civil dialogue in which all members of the community can participate. Social infrastructure encourages and reinforces expected and accepted behavior that protects, cares for, and enhances the well-being of the community and its individual members. Restoration of community means rebuilding its physical, economic, and social infrastructure. Restoring community is a circular process: it is restoring peace and safety; it is restoring the physical environment; it is restoring economic opportunity, social comity and political discourse; it is creating a polis. Each part feeds upon the other parts.

Much of the poverty in America is concentrated in places where the physical, economic, and social life of the community is deteriorated or destroyed. The prevailing public mythology is that great effort and expenditure has been focused on these places and that nothing works, nothing can be done to reverse negative conditions and rebuild neighborhoods, create opportunity, and restore the social infrastructure of community. This is simply not true. The fact is that much has been learned and accomplished in the last generation and much is being and can be done if the will and commitment is forthcoming from within these communities and from the larger society.

A Story of Rebirth in the Nation's Capital

The story of one such devastated community and its rebirth can be found in the nation's capital. This community was described by the national media as a "murderous, filthy, broken down slum." The neighborhood, known as Paradise at Parkside, is located less than two miles from the Capitol of the United States. The community is approximately 6,000 people in an area which was developed over several generations. Beginning in the 1920s, families began settling in the area, buying lots for home-building and escaping the slums and alley dwellings of segregated Washington, D.C. Apartments and shops for an emerging black middle class were built by African-Americans and supported by a strong black church organization in the 1940s and 1960s. However, by the mid-1980s, breakdown of the social, economic, and physical infrastructure brought chaos and despair to the community. The combination of joblessness, drugs, and crime overwhelmed the neighborhood. Housing was in a physically deteriorated condition. The neighborhood was under siege from drug dealing and it had become the largest and most violent open-air drug market in the region. Children could not play outside or walk to school in safety. Police were reluctant to come into the neighborhood. There were calls for the National Guard. Almost everyone with the opportunity to move out did so. Most had no choice but to stay. Some had the courage to stay and take a stand for the community.

Transformation

Over the last decade, from 1985 to 1995, the community has been transformed. Its physical infrastructure has been rebuilt; its economy has improved with opportunities for jobs, education, training, new business development; and, most importantly, its social infrastructure has been restored. This was and is being accomplished through the participation of many neighborhood residents and action by neighborhood institutions. Commitment and investment of the larger community has also been forthcoming. The public sector, at both the local and federal levels, committed resources. Members of the private sector, including developers, businesses, and philanthropic organizations have been active participants and investors.

The Paradise at Parkside transformation has been brought about through a progressive partnership among the people who live in the community, its organizations, and the public and private sectors of the larger community which participated in an inclusive planning and investment process to bring about change. The joint effort has carried out a comprehensive redevelopment of the area:

- Renovation of all 1,700 multi-family housing units in the community.
- Public housing home ownership conversion by the Kenilworth-Parkside Resident Management Corporation.
- Planned cooperative conversion of rental housing by the Paradise Resident Cooperative Corporation.
- The restoration of garden apartment complexes creating open

space designed for community recreation and interaction.

- Development of community facilities including a community center, day-care center, laundry, and learning center.
- Creation of new home ownership opportunities for moderate-income home buyers; 100 homes have been completed, over 130 more are in development.
- Retail, commercial, and health facilities created and planned.
- Employment and training programs.
- Youth mentoring and college bound programs.
- Partnership between residents and police in a successful community policing program.

Restoring Peace and Safety

The beginning of the transformation was the commitment to restore peace and safety to the community and rebuild its social infrastructure. Before any physical or economic rebuilding could take place the problem of drugs and violence had to be addressed. It was confronted by an alliance of community residents, citizen patrols by members of the Nation of Islam whose Mosque was located in the neighborhood, businesses, public agencies, and the media. The attention of the media was captured when a local drug dealer, walking through the neighborhood with his sawed-off shotgun, was confronted by an unarmed Nation of Islam citizen patrol. In the scuffle that ensued, the drug dealer was disarmed and a local reporter covering the story was caught in the melee. As a result, media attention stayed focused on the neighborhood. This incident turned out to be a transforming event. It made people aware that the problems flowing from drugs in the community could be confronted, challenged, and turned back. The community rallied and consistent opposition from residents and their supporters forced drug dealing out of the neighborhood. The drug activity left the community, dispersed, and never reconcentrated. The community's victory lead to further alliances which brought economic and physical redevelopment.

Today, comprehensive neighborhood redevelopment, including a successful community policing program which created a partnership between residents and police, has resulted in a stunning turnaround in the quality of life and the peace and safety of the community.

Since 1987, the height of crime and violence at Paradise at Parkside, the crime rate has dropped significantly. Cocaine distribution dropped from 700 incidents to less than 10; robbery from 33 to

5; shootings from 47 to 2; homicide from 6 to 0; burglary from 60 to 8; destruction of property from 42 to 12; auto theft from 60 to 15; disorderly conduct from 775 to 75; juvenile crime from 21 to 8; and person carrying a weapon from 123 to 5. This extraordinary reduction in crime demonstrates the value of effective, smart public investment and committed public/private partnerships.

Homes, Jobs, and Education

The Paradise at Parkside community has attracted over $50 million in both public and private investment. A Washington-based community development company, Telesis Corporation, organized a wide array of public and private lenders and investors to redevelop existing housing and to build new homes. The Trust for Public Land, a national nonprofit land conservation organization, played an important role as an interim land owner for the construction of new homes. The AFL-CIO Housing Investment Trust provided over $10 million in pension fund investment for rehabilitation and new home construction. The Federal National Mortgage Association (Fannie Mae) provided over $11 million in a mortgage-backed security to guarantee the pension fund investment as well as direct financing. Private investors provided over $2 million in equity investment in return for tax benefits. Local banks have provided over $10 million in home mortgages to new home buyers and will continue to finance home ownership as more homes are built. Fannie Mae is providing construction financing for new homes. NationsBank, Riggs Bank, and an insurance group are looking at the possibility of new long-term financing for further neighborhood development.

While the private sector has been a strong and effective partner in neighborhood revitalization, the role of the public sector has been critical to success as well.

Local government provided funding for the development of new infrastructure: streets, sidewalks, water and sewer connections. Over $3 million of local funds were invested in these essential building blocks. Local government also provided loan guarantees for home construction funding. Local agencies were partners in establishing and staffing a day-care center and an after school learning center.

The federal government was a critical partner in many ways. Federal funds were made available to local government for physical development through the national community development block grant program. The federal government provided mortgage guarantees to home buyers as well as "soft" second mortgages to make home ownership more affordable. Low-interest loans were also provided. Grants were provided by the federal government to build the community facilities, including the day care, community, and learning centers. And federal funds were provided to conduct employment, training, and education programs which resulted in over 100 residents being placed in jobs, including jobs created by the ongoing construction at Paradise at Parkside.

Job training and education services included personal evaluations; career/skill aptitude assessment; job coaching and peer group support; job placement; personal credit and financial planning; basic skill training and referral in math, reading, and writing; and comprehensive referral services for off-site employment skill training, health maintenance, and family support services.

To address the concerns neighborhood residents held for their youth, a number of educational, social, and cultural programs for residents were developed by public and private sponsors and the residents.

Young People On the Rise (YPOR), begun in 1987 by twenty-seven youth, is a student-run program for junior and senior high school students. Students elect their own officers and plan much of their schedule of activities. YPOR provides educational, leadership, and career opportunities and training, with a special focus on self-esteem, cultural awareness, college entrance skill, and college enrollment.

The Paradise Learning Center is open during the school year on weekdays. It provides drop-in individual and group tutoring, computer training, and other activities. It is operated by the D.C. Public Schools and is staffed by a D.C. teacher and two teacher assistants. The After-School Program gives young children the opportunity to read, watch movies, and play board games.

There is a Paradise Day Care Center, run by the D.C. Department of Recreation and Parks. It is open weekdays and offers Day Care and Headstart. Health and health-related concerns are served by: the Abundant Life Clinic, a private clinic, which offers a wide variety of progressive health services, including general medical examinations, weight loss, nutrition counseling, and HIV and AIDS treatment; D.C. Healthy Start, a program designed to reduce the rate of infant mortality, which is particularly high in this section of the city; and Narcotics Anonymous, a support group for those who have overcome narcotic addition and are dedicated to leading drug-free lives.

Building Social Infrastructure — Inclusive Planning

The restoration of the Paradise at Parkside community was influenced by a community-wide process that helped shape the programs and the overall direction of the development. Throughout the process, the Paradise/Parkside Community Consultant Board, which included neighborhood residents, a representative of a local city council member, neighborhood commissioners, tenant management, civic organization officials, and directors of community services and development corporations, conceived and designed major components of the Paradise/Parkside Master Plan. The Paradise/Parkside Master Plan set the policy and timetable for the entire project, thereby empowering the community to determine which community needs would be addressed first.

To further identify community needs and to encourage community-wide communication, the Board organized half a dozen focus groups to hold discussions on topics of vital interest to the community.

The group advanced three major themes. *First*, there was grave concern over danger in the neighborhood. *Second*, there was a need for adequate services, including educational, medical, and social services, and retail and commercial business. *Third*, there was a desire for self-determination in the development process.

The Paradise/Parkside Community Consultant Board helped to form a new social infrastructure for the community. In addition, the determination of residents to confront drug dealing and the violence it brought to the community led to new relationships, including a profound partnership with police and other law enforcement authorities in efforts to clean up the neighborhood.

The lessons learned during this period were formally incorporated into a community policing program called Koban. Started in 1994, the Koban at Paradise is based on Japan's implementation of the old neighborhood beat cop. Metropolitan Police Department officers live and work full time in the neighborhood. The police officers serve as mentors, confidants, and counselors to the residents, with a special focus on youth. The Koban community space serves as a safe haven for youth and functions as a resource and service referral center for all residents. Family counseling and support for youth are central to the Koban concept.

The combination of resident involvement, police activism, work by members of the local mosque of the Nation of Islam, and the Koban project has been remarkably effective.

Guiding Principles

The Paradise at Parkside community development is illustrative of other successful efforts around the country to restore community. One such project is located in Cleveland, Ohio. Called the Renaissance Village, this renovated 90-unit portion of the 1,021 unit King-Kennedy Project, in one of the poorest neighborhoods, has been amazing. The planning used a concept called defensible space; the following ten applications are at the heart of the idea:

- Subdivided this estate into villages.
- Offered recreation at local facility.
- Designed walkways to allow for a variety of uses.
- Provided new opportunities for children to play.
- Improved overall appearance.
- Provided each unit with its own front door, eliminating interior public space in each building.
- Cut off vehicular access for interior zones.
- Constructed a six-foot-high perimeter fence.
- Involved residents and management in the design.
- Set up areas to promote social interaction.[64]

Successes are happening everyday and they share common guiding principles:

- Human potential is the most valuable community asset.
- Investments in programs and activities which enrich human potential have a positive return—the benefit is greater than the cost; education and training are the primary means to economic independence and empowerment.
- Effective programs depend on motivated, competent people providing sustained personal attention to achieve a positive outcome.
- Communities and people must have a meaningful role in planning and taking initiatives to benefit them and their neighborhoods.

The public should be made aware of the enormous success of many programs underway in communities throughout the United States: to redevelop neighborhoods, repair and build new physical infrastructure including, decent, affordable housing and necessary community facilities such as day care, community and learning centers; to train, educate, and counsel people to be productive members of the work force and the community; to restore peace and safety to communities through community policing and other innovative programs; and of the many other efforts that are restoring the physical, social, and economic life of communities through public and private partnerships. This is not well known. The public perception is that "nothing works" and that public investment in these areas can have little or no beneficial effect. The public needs to be educated to the fact that partnerships of public and private action and investment have been successful in changing negative conditions in communities and that positive returns have resulted.

A small, but representative, example of such a partnership is the "Stay-in-School" program operating in Dade County, Florida. The Stay-in-School program is funded by the Dade County Public School System and the Florida Private Industry Council. This is a program that provides counseling and summer jobs to high-school students at risk of dropping out. Young people who do not finish high school are twice as likely to be unemployed as those who graduate; three and a half times more likely to be arrested; six times more likely to be unwed parents; and seven times more likely to be welfare dependent. Avoiding the negative costs associated with dropping out is critical to the community and finishing high school is critical to individual accomplishment. The Stay-in-School program has been in operation for eight years and has served over 8,000 at-risk students. It has reduced the drop-out rate among these students from 60 percent to under 8 percent. It has a 93 percent success rate and it costs approximately $2,200 per student per year, a fraction of the negative costs that would be incurred if the student dropped out. The heart of the program is counseling and mentoring of young people by caring individuals provided through over forty community organizations throughout the county. The Stay-in-School program demonstrates that outcomes can be changed dramatically for the better with a relatively small investment. There are hundreds of such examples. Yet, these stories are not being told and funding for such programs is being cut back.

The negative costs of deteriorated communities and wasted lives are significant. The Bush administration once estimated that the costs of conditions such as incarceration, illiteracy, unemployment, and bad housing are in excess of $750 billion dollars annually. The public needs to be made aware that there are cheaper solutions.

We must revive meaningful public policy discussions about what is working, at what cost, with what positive results as part of a new National Conversation about creating positive change, expanding opportunity, opening doors to better education and jobs, and improving the quality of life for all citizens, including those stuck in impoverished communities.

Grassroots planning and activism should be supported and reinforced. The last twenty-five years have witnessed the rise of over 2,000 neighborhood organizations all over America, grounded in and dedicated to the revitalization of their communities. This grassroots revolution has begun to take off and needs to be supported by the larger community with attention, resources, and alliances.

Foundations, for example, can be much more supportive of these organizations which deliver an array of services and carry out redevelopment work at the community level. Particularly in the area of housing, neighborhood development corporations can benefit from Program Related Investments from foundations which would provide needed seed capital and predevelopment costs for community projects. Such investments would be repaid from construction and permanent financing obtained by the development corporation. While some foundations have been a source of such capital, many others could be.

The public sector, particularly the federal government, should be a more efficient, effective, and stronger partner with citizens and the private sector in the restoration of America's communities. Although the loudest political rhetoric today is calling for diminishing or eliminating the role of government in many areas, government is and must continue to be a source of investment and a financing partner. Poor communities are not spread generally across America, but are concentrated and often comprise a large part of a particular political jurisdiction. Therefore, local tax dollars are often not available from a broad and diverse tax base, but confined to the tax base of the poor community. This severely limits public resources at the local level. As a result, municipal services and investment in public infrastructure, for example, decline or do not get made. No nation can be great without great cities. A discussion of urban policy must return to the national dialogue and the withdrawal of resources from urban communities by the federal government must be reversed.

A new base for rebuilding HUD into a stronger partner can be found in the work carried out by almost five hundred communities all over America in response to HUD's call for the creation of Empowerment Zones. Empowerment Zones, created by federal legislation in 1993, were intended to focus attention on distressed urban and rural communities and to engage communities in the development of comprehensive strategic plans to link economic, physical, and human development reflecting all of the community's needs. Hundreds of communities undertook this grassroots planning effort involving wide citizen participation to produce strategic plans. The plans were comprehensive in identifying issues, needs, resources, opportunities, short-term and long-term goals, a vision of the community's future, and a timetable and plan for implementation. These plans, which were submitted to HUD in June of 1994, contain a wealth of information about how communities saw themselves and what they believed needed to be done to bring about their restoration. Only nine communities were selected for the Empowerment Zone program, but the process engaged in by ordinary citizens and local leaders all over America resulted in these plans. They were produced from the "bottom up," and should be used to structure public policy, a new HUD, and the public-private partnerships needed to carry out the plans. HUD and others working with HUD, perhaps through a foundation or university, could analyze, organize, and publish the information that came out of this remarkable planning process to guide future activity, investment and planning.

A Model For Citizen-Led Neighborhood Planning

Citizen-led community planning can be an effective means to building social infrastructure. It is also a way for a community to access successful programs so as not to "re-invent the wheel." A model for resident-led neighborhood planning for community restoration projects is currently being used for redevelopment of the Ellen Wilson neighborhood in Washington, D.C., This neighborhood is a racially and economically diverse community that is planning the redevelopment of an abandoned public housing project in the heart of Capitol Hill. This planning model, developed by the Youth Policy Institute of Washington, D.C., is premised on the belief that a community united around a common history and core set of common values can achieve significant and lasting change in even the most distressed neighborhoods. Real community involvement is a vital component of any plan. The plan must not only be supported by local residents and organizations, but must be actually shaped by them. Therefore, the goal is simple: to provide residents the opportunity to shape the programs that will benefit their families and their community.

The centerpiece of the neighborhood planning process is the convening of bimonthly "town meetings." In the early stages, neighborhood residents discuss the common issues that are of concern to the community, such as crime, economic development, health care, and education. In each area, residents work to identify the specific problems that they want to see addressed, and engage in a dialogue to set consensus goals for the community.

At later town meetings, discussions move from dialogue to decision-making. A team of "resident facilitators" lead their fellow residents through a series of strategic planning sessions. The facilitators are members of the community engaged in hands-on leadership training. Issue by issue, the community looks at its problems, looks at the goals it has set, and looks at the options for solving those problems and meeting those goals.

The planning process includes two additional steps. First, the Comprehensive Objective Research on Policy Solutions (CORPS) brings together a baseline of local and national information that is presently not available. Second, this structured information is made available in a way that empowers residents to make real decisions about what will be implemented in the community.

The CORPS

Local university students participating in an unique service/learning project provide the information that makes this planning possible. CORPS students are trained in an "action research" methodology. This methodology enables them to analyze programs systematically.

The CORPS researcher will complete a "Taking Stock" and a "Best Practices" analysis. The "Taking Stock" analysis will be both a needs assessment and a hard examination of demographic data and existing programs in the targeted neighborhood. The "Best Practices" analysis will be an examination of model programs locally and nationwide in the issue areas that residents have identified.

Once both analyses have been completed, residents will know the extent of the problems in their neighborhood, the current programs and their scope, the cost, and the concrete options available for meeting service gaps and needs.

Resident Facilitators and the Empowernet

The role of the "resident facilitators" is to organize, motivate, and energize the community: organize residents to participate in the planning process; motivate residents to tackle complex issues and work towards consensus; energize the neighborhood to support and implement the final plan.

To complement the planning process a community-based computer network called Empowernet will be established. Empowernet is an advanced database and communications network that will be connected to the YPI database and will also house the CORPS analyses. Empowernet will serve as an on-line bulletin board and a tool for interactive participation and will be linked to local organizations and sites at libraries and public schools.

Capacity-Focused Approach

At the core of community restoration is how one approaches communities. It is obvious that the Task Force approach is one of optimism. The positive attributes of these communities are the citizens who live and work there. One of the most essential areas for restoring communities is an adequate assessment of the community itself and for that we recommend the work of Dr. John L. McKnight of the Center for Urban Affairs and Policy Research at Northwestern University. This excerpt from the work *Mapping Community Capacity* by McKnight and John P. Krutzman expresses the approach that is endorsed by this Task Force when working with low-income communities.

Traditional Needs-Oriented Solutions

This approach is accepted by most elected officials who codify and program this perspective through deficiency-oriented policies and programs. Then, human service systems—often supported by foundations and universities—translate the programs into local activities that teach people the nature of their problems, and the value of services as the answer to their problems.

As a result, many low-income urban neighborhoods are now environments of service where behaviors are affected because residents come to believe that their well-being depends upon being a client. They see themselves as people with special needs to be met by outsiders.

[This] is the predictable course of events when deficiency and needs-oriented programs come to dominate the lives of neighborhoods.

The Capacity-Focused Alternative

The alternative is to develop policies and activities based on the capacities, skills, and assets of low-income people and their neighborhoods.

There are two reasons for this capacity-oriented emphasis. First, all the historic evidence indicates that significant community development only takes place when local community people are committed to investing themselves and their resources in the effort.

The second reason for emphasizing the development of the internal assets of local urban neighborhoods is that there is very little prospect that large-scale industrial or service corporations will be locating in these neighborhoods. Nor is it likely that significant new inputs of federal money will be forthcoming soon. Therefore, it is increasingly futile to wait for significant help to arrive from outside the community. The hard truth is that development must start from within the community and, in most of our urban neighborhoods, there is no other choice.

Unfortunately, the dominance of the deficiency-oriented social service model has led many people in low-income neighborhoods to think in terms of local needs rather than assets. These needs are often identified, quantified, and mapped by conducting "needs surveys." The result is a map of the neighborhood's illiteracy, teenage pregnancy, criminal activity, drug use, etc.

But in neighborhoods where there are effective community development efforts, there is also a map of the community's assets, capacities, and abilities. For it is clear that even the poorest city neighborhood is a place where individuals and organizations represent resources upon which to rebuild. The key to neighborhood regeneration is not only to build upon those resources which the community already controls, but to harness those that are not yet available for local development purposes.[65]

RECOMMENDATIONS

The Task Force recommends:

- The public be made aware of the enormous success of many programs under way in communities throughout the United States: to develop neighborhoods, repair and build new physical infrastructure including decent, affordable housing and necessary community facilities such as day-care, community, and learning centers; to train, educate, and counsel people to be productive members of the work force and the community; to restore peace and safety to communities through community policing and other innovative programs; and of the many other efforts that are restoring the physical, social, and economic life of communities through public and private partnerships. The public must be educated to the fact that partnerships of public and private action and investment have been successful in changing negative conditions in communities and that positive returns have resulted.

• The Paradise at Parkside model developed in Washington, D.C., should be replicated in five selected communities around the country.

• Grassroots planning and activism be supported and reinforced. The last twenty-five years have witnessed the rise of over 2,000 neighborhood organizations all over America, grounded in and dedicated to the revitalization of their communities. This grassroots revolution has begun to take off and needs to be supported by the larger community with attention, resources, and alliances. Foundations, for example, can be much more supportive of these organizations which deliver an array of services and carry out redevelopment work at the community level.

• Foundations can also fund neighborhood planning efforts to be undertaken as described in this report.

• The public sector, particularly the federal government, should be a more efficient, effective, and stronger partner with citizens and the private sector in the restoration of America's communities. Although the loudest political rhetoric today is calling for diminishing or eliminating the role of government in many areas, government is and must continue to be a source of investment and a financing partner.

CIVIC DIALOGUE

A new national dialogue must ask the following questions: What are we trying to communicate when we talk about African-American men and boys individually and collectively and their troubles in this society? What are we saying about black boys today and why? What do they symbolize in American public dialogue today? But, we must also ask what will constitute a new civic dialogue, and how can a new civic journalism help to support that work? The issue here is to build capacity through dialogue and to eliminate hate and mistrust.

Background

This theme—the creation of a constructive national conversation, a new civic dialogue—undergirds all the other themes that have emerged from the National Task Force on African-American Men and Boys.

America cannot create a widespread sense of polis, public kinship, or the common good without a new national dialogue. Obviously, we cannot engage in civic storytelling without such a conversation. And we will never reinvent civil and economic life, or restore community-based leadership and community institutions, until we learn how to talk about them while transcending hatred and mistrust, and then reach some broad-based understanding of how we can achieve the objectives we all seek.

Unilateral or monoracial attempts to implement virtually every one of the many excellent recommendations of the Task Force cannot change America in any substantial way. And substantial change is essential if the current plight of African-American boys and men—or indeed, that of entire black communities—is ever to be alleviated. Anything less than a new national dialogue must leave our communities in substantially the same deplorable condition we find them in today.

Indeed, some critics may contend that virtually every other recommendation of the National Task Force on African-American Men and Boys has been attempted, in some fashion, in some recent year, somewhere in the nation's black community. What is different—what must be different, if we are to succeed this time—is that the Task Force's recommendations are projected for implementation within the context of a new national awareness and understanding.

That awareness, that understanding, can occur only if the Task Force's call for a new national dialogue is heeded and fully developed. In the absence of the effort, resources, and success implied by that statement, America's black community will not be—*cannot be*—substantially affected by the work of the Task Force.

So let us begin with an understanding of what we mean by a new national dialogue. We do not mean more typical talk radio, or more pundits battling each other through newspaper editorials. We do not mean national politicians presuming to speak for the rest of us.

When we recommend enhanced national dialogue concerning issues of race in America, we mean individuals—both so-called spokespeople and millions of regular citizens, formally and informally—interacting, actively listening to each other's interests, and together developing solutions to common problems. By "national" we suggest that such dialogue must be so extensive, and so valued, that it becomes widely visible, so widely known that it begins to change expectations and then norms of public behavior.

We seek, ultimately, the impact of public dialogue on civic culture, and thus on public behavior—on public policies as well as action within American communities.

The Obstacles

Can America achieve this much-needed new national dialogue? Many would argue that a constructive dialogue is impossible. Moral leadership has given way to activities by some individuals who espouse clever slogans and use divisive labels. The Civil Rights

Movement is stuck in process, in trying to reverse judicial rulings, while harsh economic realities force millions of workers, black and white, to claw for the same jobs. Exhaustion has set in, a sense of disappointment and failure. After more than two decades of Affirmative Action programs, polls show that a large proportion of whites feel that the playing field has been leveled, if not tilted against them. Yet most blacks still feel they are the victims of discrimination, and there never has been greater disagreement about whether past discrimination entitles blacks to preference in education or hiring. While the rawest forms of racial prejudice are in decline, many political leaders have made a science of subtle polarization.

But the huge problems are not confined to the political arena, of course. America's colleges and universities—to take but one of the many possible examples—were once considered havens of tolerance. Although they were presumably enlightened, and presumably liberal, they have become laboratories for social antagonism. And, as is typical of so many sectors of American society in recent years, progress has been minimal, at best. Twenty years ago, 6.6 percent of all master's degrees went to blacks. Now only about 4.6 percent are awarded to African-Americans. Blacks received 4.3 percent of all professional degrees in 1976, and now they are receiving 4.4 percent. Doctoral degrees awarded to blacks have declined about 20 percent in the past decade. If higher education furnishes a key strategy to chiseling away at racial barriers, only a long-term perspective offers grounds for optimism.

The results of two decades of attempts to increase racial diversity on the nation's campuses are mirrored in every major institution throughout American society. At many levels, both races continue to resist the forces and programs that support integration in housing, employment, even human services. Whites with their rationales for not mixing more with blacks, blacks with their rhetoric of separatism and narrow "community development," still keep to themselves, to their own race, in large numbers.

A number of recent studies document the phenomenon of continued American segregation—and, by implication, also demonstrate how hard it will be to build a new national dialogue based on honesty and a willingness to transcend hatred. Most notable of these recent books is Andrew Hacker's *Two Nations: Black and White, Separate, Hostile, Unequal*. Hacker demonstrates that no other minority group has made so unavailing a struggle for acceptance, finding at the root of the disenfranchisement of black Americans the disabling but subtle and pervasive misconceptions of profound, deep-seated racism (particularly the notion that blacks are inherently intellectually inferior.) As Hacker analyzes the choices all Americans, black and white, make in daily life—how we select our neighborhoods, our political candidates, our heroes and cultural icons—he demonstrates how deeply issues of race shape the thinking of all Americans. Such thinking goes to the roots of our public policies and private attitudes regarding teenage pregnancy, drugs, illiteracy, crime, unemployment, inadequate and inferior housing—and even our willingness to enter into dialogue across racial lines. So many of our cities have large poor populations, and a declining economic base, that Hacker seems to suggest that increasing, not decreasing, segregation lies in America's immediate future.

Another important study draws essentially the same conclusion. In *American Apartheid: Segregation and the Making of the Underclass*, Douglas Massey and Nancy Denton demonstrate that residential markets allocate housing, schooling, peer groups, safety, jobs, insurance costs, public services, home equity, "and, ultimately, wealth. By tolerating the persistent and systematic disenfranchisement of blacks from housing markets, we send a clear signal to one group that hard work, individual enterprise, sacrifice, and aspirations don't matter; what determines one's life chances is the color of one's skin."[66]

Their fundamental argument is that racial segregation—and its characteristic institutional form, the black inner cities, with its nearly insurmountable barriers to black-white dialogue—are the key structural factors responsible for the perpetuation of black poverty (and the urban underclass) in the United States.

Hacker, Massey, and Denton all make the same case: there is substantial, perhaps growing, apartheid in many sectors of American society. That view is further reinforced by such books as *Jews and Blacks*, by Michael Lerner and Cornell West, and *From Cradle to Grave: The Human Face of Poverty in America*, by Jonathan Freedman. The former presents a strong sense of growing, not shrinking, resentment among interracial groupings that were formerly considered allies, and the latter reveals the hardships, the nearly incalculable odds, confronting America's poor—along with the courage and the hope they continue to display.

And these books imply the three preliminary points we wish to make concerning the development of a national dialogue.

First, let us be clear about our aim. Broad prosperity in America has always resided in the mainstream. (This is why the Afrocentric/Eurocentric debate often misses the point). And the only way, ultimately, to dissolve racial differences—and create the prosperity that the Task Force calls for—is for more blacks to join the mainstream, while more whites welcome them in. That conclusion most emphatically does *not* mean that we accept uncritically much about the mainstream, or that we do not believe that much about mainstream practices require reform or change. We mean only that whites will dominate most key American institutions for a long time to come. And for all the frustrations, working within those institutions—while working to change them—is in all likelihood the surest way for large numbers of blacks to better their condition. That can be accomplished only through dialogue—broad-based and wide-scale, bi-racial and multi-class, honest and frank.

Second, Americans still support the *ideal* of integration and dialogue. In one national poll, 72 percent of blacks and 52 percent of whites say they would prefer to live in a neighborhood that is racially "half and half." That actually represents an *increase* in pro-integration sentiment over several years. While the hard economic evidence indicates that white Americans will begin to move out of neighborhoods that pass a threshold of 8 to 10 percent black, they still maintain their belief that a multicultural neighborhood is desirable for a variety of reasons. Indeed, additional evidence points to this simple conclusion regarding the possibility of a sustained, serious national dialogue on matters of race: Americans, both black and white, don't associate in large numbers with those of other races, but they believe they would *like* to. Most believe such dialogue is desirable for ethical and moral reasons. They also think it is preferable for their children, as well as for the future of this nation and our society. We may practice Balkanization and apartheid in our dialogues, but we do not approve of our current practices.

Third, our last preliminary point is that some African-Americans, following the lead of the worst elements of white America, both willingly and unwittingly play into the hands of segregationists who would quash all dialogue at every opportunity. Massey and Denton point to segregation for the creation of "an oppositional culture that devalues work, schooling and marriage." One of the central attributes of that culture is what could be called a no-fault attitude, a conviction that "nothing I do is my fault, since white men created the awful conditions in which I must live. It was not black Americans, after all, who decided to segregate cities and leave the worst neighborhoods to blacks."

So, as a matter of integrity, we want to be very honest concerning the dialogical apartheid we are confronting when we call for a new national dialogue. Some whites resist a new national dialogue, to be sure; we can be certain that we will always find white racists among us who blindly oppose black-white dialogue as well as mono-cultural dialogues concerning racial matters. But some blacks also are sufficiently racist to oppose the dialogues we call for here. Their opposition stems from a variety of needs that they feel cannot be addressed by the white community. We believe they are partially incorrect in their analyses, understandably afraid, and unfortunately shortsighted. They also do not understand the significant failures that their approaches have registered thus far in the black communities of our nation.

We began this section on obstacles with the following question: "Can America achieve the much-needed new national dialogue?" We've said that it is indeed much needed—that the progress America and America's blacks require in every important area is quite literally inconceivable without it. And we've suggested that the achievement may be possible—even in the face of worsening trends—because Americans still want it. But we have also maintained that important portions of both the white and black communities do *not* want such a national conversation, and that, therefore, a realistic analysis suggests, at best, a tempered optimism in the face of considerable obstacles. We can indeed break down dialogical apartheid, and create the national conversation America needs, but only when the appropriate variety of resources, as well as the appropriate magnitude of resources, are made available to address this pressing and most critical need.

Some Notes on the Nature of Public Dialogue

We begin this section with an important note: public dialogue defined simply as talk is decidedly not what we are after. We said that public dialogue, to be useful, must have an impact—it must alter and improve the civic culture and then lead to changes in public policies and public behavior.

This is why, in our recommendations, we place so much emphasis on the media, on the means by which nearly all Americans receive a large proportion of the key messages circulating within our society.

But in this section of our report, we want to discuss other aspects of the nature of public dialogue, aspects which are often overlooked and yet also are key determinants of the useful quality of public dialogue. Dialogue must impact values and behavior, to be sure, and therefore lead to public action, but it must also have other qualities.

Benjamin Barber, in the book entitled *Strong Democracy*, describes what we mean by "civic culture" as "common consciousness." He observes that "the first and most significant phase" of developing a civic culture is that of talk—dialogue in various forms. He asserts that dialogue "lies at the heart of strong democracy," and includes both speaking and listening, cognition as well as affect, agenda-setting, the formation of issues, the identification and articulation of interests, public decision-making, and the realization that common talk must lead to common work and common action.

With dialogue, Barber states, "We can invent alternative futures, create mutual purposes, and construct competing visions of community. . . . [Such] talk is not talk *about* the world; it is talk that makes and remakes the world."[67]

Such talk is useful only when it is disciplined by what Harry Boyte, who addressed the Task Force, has termed "skillful public action." Thus public dialogue, as we use the term in Task Force discussions, implies skilled communication, skilled listening, and the variety of "arts of democracy" referred to by Frances Moore Lappé and by Paul Martin DuBois, who also addressed the Task Force. These ten skills of democratic engagement, described in Moore Lappé and DuBois' book, *The Quickening of America: Remaking Our Nation, Remaking Our Lives*, must be learned by those who want public dialogue to become widespread and effective. Such functional public arts as mediation, negotiation, creative conflict, and evaluation all enrich public dialogue immensely.

So when we talk about *serious* public dialogue, we are discussing dialogue between whites and blacks—and among blacks as well as among whites, meeting separately—concerning such key topics as race relations. The *quality* of the dialogue successfully addresses the several common objections to such public dialogue as "just talk," or "all talk and no action," or "another way of selling out." Here, as Barber sees them, are the nine functions of "strong democratic talk."

These characteristics, in our perspective, determine the quality of public dialogue and can render it fully effective and highly useful.

- Public dialogue encourages the articulation of interests, even bargaining and exchange among interests. Earlier we described the importance, within the democratic model, of identifying and understanding self-interests in accurate, open and candid fashion. True public dialogue acknowledges and makes use of those understandings as they are developed and expressed.
- Public dialogue supports attempts at persuasion, which should be, after all, the application of human reasoning to issues of judgment and value.
- Public dialogue encourages involvement in public agenda-setting, or determining priorities for public decision-making and public action.
- Public dialogue enables us to explore much more than merely our differences. We are searching for mutually beneficial exchanges, after all, and public dialogue permits discovery of both divergent interests and mutual interests. It also permits us to transcend simplistic definitions of complex relationships, so that we learn to air choices and exchange benefits with people who are seen as far more complex than simple adversaries.
- Public dialogue permits us to know and understand one another. Sometimes we may even like what we discover. When we convey information, articulate interests, and pursue arguments, we can feel and affect each other, thereby reassuring, frightening, comforting, intimidating, soothing, and even loving one another.
- Public dialogue permits us to maintain autonomy, buttressing our capacities to encounter, evaluate, and strengthen the beliefs and principles that matter most to us.
- Public dialogue also undergirds the autonomous person by strengthening one's place in a public community while leaving room for the expression of distrust or dissent.
- Public dialogue helps us change and grow, challenging our views and enabling us to add information to previous formulations.
- Public dialogue also permits community building because it helps both develop and create public interests as well as active citizens. As Barber puts it, "All the functions of talk . . . converge toward a single, crucial end—the development of a citizenry capable of genuinely public thinking and political judgment and thus able to envision a common future in terms of genuinely common goods."[68]

These characteristics of public dialogue underscore our use of the word *serious*; we are discussing very serious talk, talk that carries profound consequences and produces impacts.

Such talk, after decades of struggle and debate throughout American society, led this nation to develop a broad consensus regarding what we are against concerning the races. We reject slavery, deliberate discrimination, legal segregation. But we have not yet decided what we are *for*, nor have we determined, in many cases, how we are best going to achieve whatever goals we set.

We believe that it is the absence of genuine public dialogue, including the absence of forthright discussions of self-interest, that have left many Americans in a murky realm in which they can oppose certain forms of outright racial discrimination but do not fully understand what they *do* stand for and how they can expect to realize their highest values.

The Democratic Rationale for a National Interracial Dialogue

Two and one-half years ago, Task Force members met in Washington, D.C. at the African-American Males conference. In the words of the summary, the attendees realized that:

There are few issues of greater importance to the future of the United States than the plight of some African-American men and boys. A large percentage are engaged in a desperate struggle for survival—one that not only endangers their lives, but threatens the well-being of their families and their communities.

Since that time, things have gotten worse.

- A black male baby born in Los Angeles has three times as much chance being murdered as being admitted to the University of California.
- More children than ever live in poverty; in the last five years the number of children living in poverty increased by one million, to a total of over six million. And the definition of what constitutes poverty, of course, is unacceptable.
- Now 46 percent of black children live in poverty, compared to 17 percent of white children.
- One-fourth of young black males have turned to crime—they are under indictment, in jail, or on parole.
- White male teenagers are killed at a rate of 13 per 100,000. Black teenagers are killed at 92 per 100,000 each year, and that tragic figure has more than doubled in the last five years.

- In some black communities in the United States, black males are less likely to reach the age of thirty than are men in Bangladesh.
- In one single day in this country, 3,300 children run away from home; 2,800 teenagers get pregnant; 1,900 teenagers become dropouts; 1,700 children are in adult jails; and five children commit suicide every single day. And a drastically disproportionate number of them are African-American males.

The problems are worsening. The wounds are deepening. The scars are thickening. The Task Force has grappled with the fact that these problems are also *symptoms*, symptoms of deeper forces that are complex, huge, and interrelated.

And, to be effective, it is clear to the Task Force that our solutions must match the power of the problems. Thus our solutions must also be large, complex, and interrelated. They must cut beneath all the symptoms—beneath run-down housing, violence, drugs, unemployment, inadequate health care, and poor education.

The thousands of programs and billions of dollars expended to address these problems—while they continue to worsen—suggest that the solutions may lie deeper than we have heretofore been willing to acknowledge.

Perhaps we need to examine the very meaning of democracy itself—with all the power it has as both a concept and a set of practices—if we are to find the deepest, most long-lasting, most powerful solutions. Perhaps we have to reinvent democracy capable of meeting the depth and complexity of today's problems.

What's Been Tried

Let's begin by looking at the strategies that millions of people of good will have adopted thus far to free African-Americans from oppression:

THREE PRINCIPAL STRATEGIES, AND SOME KEY CHARACTERISTICS CONTRIBUTING TO SUCCESS

STRATEGY #1: CIVIL RIGHTS	STRATEGY #2: AFFIRMATIVE ACTION	STRATEGY #3: ANTIPOVERTY
Mass mobilization and involvement	Black and white collaboration and functioning as allies	Investment of resources

STRATEGY #1: CIVIL RIGHTS	STRATEGY #2: AFFIRMATIVE ACTION	STRATEGY #3: ANTI-POVERTY
Strong leaders with strong white allies. Often fighting stark injustices with legal remedies	Essentially legal and administrative strategy	Some capacity building and some problem-solving involvement by clients/recipients

In the civil rights strategy, blacks sought to outlaw discrimination, to enforce equality under the law. The goal: to force governments to fulfill their obligations to ensure equal opportunity among all individuals in voting, classrooms, public accommodations, employment, promotions, housing, etc.

In the last forty years (beginning with the 1954 Brown decision), this strategy has been a qualified success; public attitudes have shifted from majority support for segregation to majority support for equal treatment. And since the 1964 Civil Rights Act, the legal system has enforced laws barring discrimination in serving customers in restaurants, admitting students to colleges, interviewing candidates for jobs, counting votes, or selling houses.

But these laws can't remedy the effects of three hundred years of preferential treatment that one race has enjoyed over another. Many blacks realized years ago that they need a government that assumes *affirmative* obligations to remedy the long-term effects of slavery and segregation.

Thus, affirmative action. The fundamental principle is that government must require that historically discriminated-against groups receive fair treatment as measured by *results*, especially in the workplace. Some blacks have advocated temporary special benefits to compensate for centuries of disadvantages, to counter today's discrimination, and to benefit society as a whole.

Because of affirmative action, there have been significant increases in minority employment, government contracts for minorities, integrated police forces, and so on. But today's vigorous backlash against affirmative action makes its future highly doubtful.

The third strategy to address the plight of African-Americans has been to fight poverty, since blacks are disproportionately poor. Poverty-related conditions keep millions from becoming literate or economically viable. William Julius Wilson argues that "class is more important than race in determining access to power and privilege." Thirty-eight million Americans live below the poverty line— including 24 percent of all children but 46 percent of black children.

The conventional wisdom, created by a constant barrage of conservative propaganda, holds that government antipoverty programs have failed miserably. What conventional wisdom ignores is that Medicaid, food stamps, subsidized housing, Supplemental Security Income, targeted student loans, employment training all contributed to a very significant decline in poverty. During the 1960s, poverty rates fell from 22 percent to 12 percent.

Unfortunately, in the simplistic debate over whether government antipoverty programs work or don't work, the real issues are ignored: What kind of government program and at what level of funding? Clearly government programs fail unless they work directly in partnership with citizens, enabling people to gain skills and access to jobs that pay a living wage—and unless the jobs are there. We've never achieved such partnerships, funded adequately.

Our point is that blacks (and white allies) have tried these three strategies. And it's now time to learn from this history in order to create a different strategy, one that is as large and complex and interrelated as the problems we face, one that can match the force of our problems.

What hasn't been tried? In one sense, what African-Americans haven't tried is democracy, the most fundamental strategy of all. *Democracy!* The fate of African-Americans depends on the fate of America's democracy.

We've all been brought up believing we have simply inherited democracy. After all, democracy amounts to a set of formal institutions of government—our Constitution, our multiple party systems, our countervailing powers, and so on.

And more and more Americans—not simply African-Americans—feel this formal democracy is not working for them. Almost three-fourths reported recently that government is run by insiders who don't care about ordinary people and who can't solve our problems.

Most Americans feel increasing economic insecurity. Since the wealthy reaped the vast bulk of all income gains in the last fifteen years, the gap between rich and poor is wider than ever in our lifetime. The top 1 percent control as much wealth as the bottom 90 percent.

As a result, more and more of us withdraw in despair. In the last election, two-thirds of all those eligible to vote did not even bother.

It's not just minorities who feel powerless, who feel unequal, who feel they have a right to be angry. Large numbers of other

Americans feel that way, too. Their anger gets directed at "government," leading many to acquiesce to, even applaud, government cutbacks. But those cutbacks end up hurting average Americans and low-income Americans the most. And the anger of the majority gets directed at immigrants and the poor (disproportionately minorities) who are seen as drains on the public purse.

The fate of African-Americans cannot be disentangled from this downward spiral of pain, anger, blaming, and withdrawal from public engagement.

African-Americans can emerge into full citizenship only as we reverse this cycle by creating a democracy that works for all of us, in which we are all full citizens. Such a democracy—a process of successful problem solving—is much, much more than our formal institutions. To address the terrible crisis of race, we as a people must take that next step in the ongoing historical creation of democracy. Some of us call that step "living democracy."

Regardless of what names we use for the type of democracy we need, it is clear that America desperately needs to improve its civic culture. Beneath every social structure is a culture—the set of values, attitudes, expectations, and assumptions about the contributions of ordinary people in making public choices. To create a culture of democracy requires serious rethinking, rethinking the meaning of such core concepts and practices as public life, power, and what it takes to be an effective citizen. That rethinking is the key, underlying purpose for creating a new, nationwide civic dialogue.

And, as we've just noted, that national dialogue must include—implicitly or explicitly—certain understandings of key concepts.

Public Life

Today most assume that public life is only what officials and celebrities have. But in the emerging practice of more effective democracy, thousands of Americans are learning that we each have a public life. It includes every aspect of our lives outside our bedrooms—from the schools we and our children attend to our ties to government policies, from our relationship to employers who hire us (and the ones who don't) to the media that stream into our living rooms and into our children's minds for hundreds and hundreds of hours, year after year.

This understanding of the concept of public life may sound obvious, but it is a radical notion for many people. It suggests capacities and responsibilities that most of us have believed we had to (or should) leave to others.

Prior strategies for addressing racism and discrimination did not include this core message—that we each can and should have a voice in all of these arenas. The assumption was that we could achieve fair access to, say, voting, or employment, and that was it. Acknowledging that we each have public lives, public roles in which we can take responsibility for decision making, suggests the need to build skills in each of us.

Power

Similarly, those creating a culture of democracy are rethinking power. Typically, strategies for social change have urged the less powerful, such as African-Americans, to seize power from the more powerful. But what successful problem solvers are learning today is that new power can be created from many, many sources. It is what we ourselves build through relationships of mutual accountability. It is not merely what we seize from others.

In the 1960s, for example, activists in the African-American community built health clinics and housing projects, and demanded money to pay for them. They focused on the structures. They focused on the victories. They didn't build relationships of mutual accountability with the other members of the community. They didn't build the capacities of the citizens involved. They didn't change the way decisions were made, or the expectations about the role of regular citizens in making public decisions.

These earlier strategies never empowered millions of people to participate fully in what could have been their democratic public lives, so that broad masses of people would be capable of running their public lives. But much has developed, and many lessons have been learned, since the 1960s—since the failure of top-down strategies to sustain improved lives for African-Americans. This stronger culture of democratic practice, democratic values, is being built today from the bottom up. True, the media are not telling us, but a revolution is taking place in hundreds of communities.

Despite the terrifying downward trends cited above, African-Americans are creating this culture of democracy in communities across America. They are claiming their public lives, creating relational power, and learning the capacities (the "arts" of democracy) for ongoing effectiveness.

Across the nation today, roughly two million Americans are involved in congregation-based organizations. Many are rooted in African-American churches united with white congregations. These networks involve their members in in-depth training in how to build relational power and how to hold themselves and others accountable for constructive outcomes. Here are a few examples:

- Shelby County Interfaith in Memphis, Tennessee, is just one example. There, thirty-five congregations, black and white, held over four hundred house meetings to listen to citizens' concerns about Memphis' failing schools. They arrived at a sophisticated school reform plan that, because it had such widespread support, was passed unanimously by the Memphis School Board. What's important here is not this "victory." What's important is that hundreds of ordinary citizens learned what they needed to know to hold officials accountable and to hold themselves accountable for design and implementation of the reform.
- YouthBuild is another lesson-filled example. The Boston-based program teaches inner city dropouts, largely African-Americans, construction skills while they get a GED. It has now spread to fourteen states, and is demonstrating striking results in changing the lives of young people.
- Or consider Cooperative Home Care in the Bronx, New York. Eighty percent of CHCA workers—roughly half African-American and half Latina—were welfare recipients who had never before worked in formal jobs. In ten years, CHCA has achieved the status of a "yardstick" company, one setting higher standards for the entire New York home health care industry. Now CHCA is being replicated in several other cities.
- Or Seattle. There the black mayor, Norm Rice, has taken the lead in the creation and growth of a Department of Neighborhoods. Its function is to animate citizens and help train them in effective problem solving. Instead of government as simply protector or provider, here government is learning to operate in partnership with citizens. And it has focused on the poorest neighborhoods with disproportionate numbers of African-Americans.

Part of the work of the Task Force was focused on young people. They are participating in this democratic revolution in important, powerful ways. Programs in the art of democracy called creative conflict are now part of the curriculum in more than 2,000 schools, and evaluations by two hundred teachers showed that within one year that type of education reduced the number of fights in classrooms by 71 percent. In Charlotte, North Carolina, teachers say that mediation reduced the number of assaults by 55 percent in just one school year.

Here are seeds of a new kind of progress—chosen from thousands like them. They represent not just specific victories but new cultural norms. Regular people are learning the skills to be creative in public life. People of color are in many cases leading initiatives toward a living democracy, in government, human services, education, workplaces, and the media.

These are different types of organizations, evolving out of the successes and failures of the 1960s, 70s and 80s. Most important, they are *learning* organizations. They have discovered a new way to advance the cause of African-Americans, and the cause of all Americans. These people are building power through building relationships that work for them.

Such examples demonstrate that once power is understood as something we can create and something derived from more than money or official status, people begin to discover any number of sources of power available to them. These sources include their own numbers, the knowledge they can dig out themselves, their vision and perseverance, and even their own humor which can move and surprise others.

Second, such examples demonstrate the power of deliberately focusing on human "capacity building." Here, citizens are practicing and learning the arts of democracy—those skills we all need in order to solve our problems and to make effective, democratic communities. Such skills as active listening, creative conflict, negotiation, evaluation, and mentoring (and many more) can be taught with all the deliberate attention and satisfaction that we devote to learning to read or write.

Beyond blame, beyond scapegoating, many Americans are creating the seeds of a more participatory, inclusive culture, which is the only path to addressing the deep crisis of Black America.

A New National Dialogue is Crucial to Continued Success and to The Spread of Democracy at the Grassroots Level

The organizations that are charting new cultural norms share certain characteristics and are asking similar questions. They are asking some of the core questions about the meaning of power and public life.

These "seeds" cannot flourish—cannot begin to reverse the frightening downward spiral of despair and withdrawal—unless they become widely known. Today they are virtually invisible. That is why several of our recommendations center on impacting the media. Such new institutions as the News Service of the Center for Living Democracy are essential for creating a new national dialogue, leading to a new civic culture that improves the ways all Americans think about key issues as well as the implied concepts of power, public life, the meaning of citizenship, and the interracial justice a majority still professes as an ideal.

In the last analysis, this argument in favor of a richer form of democracy as essential for black progress, is very simple. Realistically, resources and strategies to regenerate our neighborhoods cannot emerge from the old paradigm. That paradigm assumed large government transfers and programs developed top-down by professional planners and social workers. Those are not realistic options today. They may not even be desirable.

The only path open today, the path of living democracy, is no quick fix. It is long-term cultural renewal, building on what is already beginning: regular citizens in communities all across America who are learning to build their own capacities, learning to build partnerships with those of other races and classes based on their own legitimate self-interests.

Therein lies our hope, in the slow birth of democracy understood as the inclusive practice of citizens who are developing skills in self governance relating to every aspect of their public lives.

This birth of democracy is possible only with a new national dialogue. Many activities are under way that are making profound differences in the lives of African-American men and boys. Many programs work. There are incredible assets in our poor communities in the talents and the energies and the sheer intelligence and moral beauty of thousands of people of good will and inspiring commitment. They are right to hope, and they provide hope to all of us. They are spearheading one of the important battles in America today, and they win many battles.

But, again, these successes are invisible. America needs to learn of them, and we all need to have them replicated. This is why our recommendations include approaches to, and use of, the mainstream media, as we plan to foster a new civic dialogue throughout our nation.

When the grassroots leaders were initially brought together to dialogue on solutions to the problems of African-American men and boys and their families at the African-American Males Conference in

1992, the conference attendees said there were six priorities that America must focus on:

- Develop a stronger sense of personal responsibility.
- Bolster cultural leadership and understanding—so that we have better role models and better understanding of African-American history and culture.
- Renew spiritual values.
- Create jobs and other productive activities for African-American boys and men.
- Enhance communication among a broad range of people, so that we build much stronger communities.
- Build the capacities of communities to deal with their own problems.

Thousands of programs are doing some good because they are implementing three of those six recommendations. They are at least attempting to do the first three, and a few of them, all too few, are attempting to do the fourth.

But are they accomplishing the last two? Rarely are they fully successful, and most are not even partially successful even when they do try. And most don't even try.

We can fight battles, but we cannot win the wars until we pay attention to these last two items, for they have to do not with building successful individuals but changing the very nature of how we as a culture, as a society create the widespread opportunities and the broadly accepted values that represent fundamental change everywhere.

As long as we continue to bandage individual wounds, deliver individual services, focus on the first items on the conference's excellent 1992 list, we will never be fully successful.

Remaking our nation begins with healing our nation. We have to recover the moral center and soul of our public life. We can do that only by fostering, and fully supporting, a new national dialogue.

Three Major Themes

The 1992 African-American Males Conference stressed three themes of direct relevance to the development of a new national dialogue:

- Building the capacities of communities to deal with their own problems.
- Bolstering cultural leadership and understanding, with strong

role models and a deeper understanding of history and culture.

- Enhancing communication among people. "Talking, sharing, helping, and working together are vital to building strong communities and a healthy society."

We all understand that these themes are essential. There are many ways to influence the public culture and thereby promote an ongoing national dialogue on the status of the races in America.

RECOMMENDATIONS

The Task Force recommends that:

- A summit should be called among the nation's major media outlets—television, newspapers, and radio newscasters. We must talk with these people to get them to better understand the plight of African-American males and to discuss together how we can change some of the negative perceptions that are being portrayed about them.
- Because a summit is only a one-time affair, attended (at best) by only a small portion of the decision-makers in the nation's media, and because years of training and follow-up will be required to change behavior and thoroughly influence the nation's media, and because many media officials admit they don't even know how to cover the stories we'd like to see, or where to find such stories, support should be provided for a new national News Service that will continuously deliver appropriate stories to thousands of media outlets, thereby changing the messages and images that are delivered into the minds of millions of our fellow citizens.

   Fortunately, a new national news service is being developed by the Center for Living Democracy. It is a massive undertaking, but the American News Service, which addresses our recommendations directly, is being developed. People need models that furnish grounds for hope, for community-building, for joining with others, and for self-development.

   The new national News Service of the Center for Living Democracy is already following the Task Force recommendations regarding civic journalism, building permanent relationships with those newspapers and radio/TV newsrooms that are willing to change their coverage of key topics and engage in constructive civic storytelling and problem-solving, thereby helping develop their entire communities' problem-solving capacities.
- Support for a special focus within the News Service should be pro-

vided, perhaps a special bureau, focused on matters of race. Such an effort will research and develop stories of people involved in public problem-solving that contribute to the constructive development of race relations throughout our society. Bureau staff will build relations with the staff of thousands of newsrooms across the United States to insure widespread coverage of such stories that will influence others to abandon despair and move into constructive action.

• Training internships and fellowships should be supported, as well as training seminars and workshops for staff currently well-placed in the media, focused on the subject of race and race relations. Such people could work with the American News Service, as well as receive a wide variety of additional experiences in media organizations under the guidance of News Service staff, in order to improve coverage of race and racial matters throughout the American media.

And the 1994 Task Force meeting on African-American images suggested consideration of careers for African-Americans throughout the nation's media, including TV and film, that extend well beyond acting and on-screen presentations. Training for such careers can be fostered in a wide variety of ways through a News Service that reaches a large portion of the nation's media outlets.

• A new organization, possibly called the National Foundation for African-Americans, be created to address the plight of black males and proclaim the contributions they have made to our society. Such an organization would challenge federal and state governments to foster change relative to African-American men.

• The Study Circles Resource Center, the National Dialogues on Race, and other efforts should be supported; they and other "structures for dialogue" that directly organize dialogues concerning race and thereby challenge widespread misperceptions as they foster new understanding.

• Learning centers should be supported as they attempt to gather and distribute materials that in turn support and foster dialogues on racial matters. As the 1994 Task Force meeting on African-American images recommended, support the development of a national clearinghouse on relevant programs, literature, and other materials. The Living Democracy Learning Center is just one of several throughout the country that could support the establishment of a separate bureau to serve as a central, nationwide collection and distribution hub specifically for materials addressing racial issues.

• Create an ongoing institution focused on the creation and support of public dialogue concerning race.

A variety of needs were mentioned by Task Force members that could perhaps be met by the creation of a focused institution or program. A think tank, a permanent research program, or similar center is needed to monitor, study, plan, encourage, test, advocate, and explore the subject of cross-race dialogue and intra-race dialogue. With appropriate support, such a center—perhaps the media institute recommended by the Task Force's 1994 workshop at Fisk University on African-American images—could be operated as a branch of the Center for Living Democracy, because that Center is presently beginning some of these functions. The new effort would continuously explore ways of building effective, democratic power and increasing self-reliance among African-American communities, as well as promoting cross-race dialogue and dialogical development within the black community.

As one example, the Task Force recommends the Indianapolis program where One Hundred Black Men have been very effective sitting in on editorial board meetings of local newspapers when executives decide what stories are covered in newspapers. How can such a program—and a variety of others that foster the important work in Civil Dialogue that this nation desperately needs—be described to leaders in many other communities? In brief, how can it be improved and spread and linked to other efforts? The institution we recommend, possibly as a branch of the Center for Living Democracy, could move into action in answering such crucial questions and fostering many similar efforts in other urban areas.

Such a think tank could consider the impacts of new technology, and the information superhighway, as it engages in strategic planning to foster the benefits of such technology throughout the black community.

• The 1992 Conference on African-American Males made several recommendations that the Center for Living Democracy (or perhaps a new institution or a branch of the present Center) could implement, including training networks for community leaders, even on local, regional, and national levels; the data-based information system discussed by the Conference; regional town meetings; and the identification and further development of program models which work successfully and ought to have secure funding (adapted from *What A Piece of Work Is Man!*, edited by Dr. Bobby William Austin).

• Training should be conducted. Large numbers of community-based agencies and organizations need training in democratic effectiveness—the essential skills and such basic concepts as building new power, understanding each person's public life, defining oneself as capable of effective action, building public relationships with media and government officials, etc. The most effective training can also focus on building the indicators of democratic success that hundreds of organizations have proven are essential to building new power and playing a critical role in key decision-making.

• Approaches to specific institutions and sectors should be defined. The Task Force often discussed the benefits and limitations of making special approaches to specific institutions. Liaison persons could be trained to reach and influence colleges, school districts, media that are now practicing civic journalism, other media outlets that may be willing to permit access for purposes of building and influencing the national dialogue, a wide variety of churches, as well as community and professional associations. All of these key institutions need both encouragement and training if they are to engage actively and effectively in supporting the national dialogue that our nation requires for long-term solutions to our racial issues. All of these institutions can be encouraged to implement one of the Task Force's central recommendations: sponsoring more public meetings concerning the problems that impact the African-American community.

These institutions can also be supported in having, and making widely available, constructive literature that helps to deepen Americans' understanding of racial issues. Learning centers, such as those described above, can serve as the medium for widespread distribution of such literature. And the Task Force also feels that young people, especially on the campuses of historically black colleges and universities, should be a prime beneficiary of such a dissemination program.

• International relationships between youth and urban ghettos and youth around the world should be attempted through teleconferencing; and that these teleconference seminars would be established and run by community institutions throughout the nation.

• An international dialogue between African-American men, African men, and Afro-Europeans should be fostered, to discuss how each can be supportive of the other as they attempt to create dialogue within their national and local communities.

10 YOUTH, VIOLENCE, AND THE GLOBAL CONTEXT

YOUNG people around the world are experiencing great and excruciating change. Never before in recorded history have such drastic changes occurred in such a short period of time. In our lifetimes we have moved from an industrial-agricultural era to a technological era that demands a high level of skill, and in a time when our economic institutions seem to encourage the isolation of individuals and families.

Readers may ask why we neglected in-depth discussions of specific issues like AIDS, delinquent fathers, drug abuse and the drug economy, drive-by shootings and violence. While we refer to them throughout this report, our goal is to focus on the need for systems change, which calls for a commitment to helping the whole person and his community. Children today are trying to grow up and be the social animals that all human beings are without many of the necessary supports.

Global Violence

This report did not, as we mentioned, use violence as the platform from which to view the African-American male, even though the Task Force was well aware that violence is one of the motivating factors and the frame through which so many institutions in the nation now perceive African-American men and boys. In an article appearing in the Phoenix Gazette, Wednesday, October 27, 1993, attorney Barry Weisberg makes the following comments:

The most common image of violent gang shootings of African-American youth too often overlooks the violence in our bedrooms, living rooms and board rooms. Interpersonal and institutional violence degrades and injures tens of millions of children, women and the elderly.

Interpersonal violence includes prenatal abuse, child abuse, corporal punishment, gender violence, sexual assault, elderly abuse, racial and ethnic violence, violence against homosexuals, murder, assault, burglary, suicide, etc.

Institutional violence results from police brutality, the death penalty, contact sports, television, film, and popular music, gangs, employment, pollution, terrorism, assassinations, militarism, riots, etc. any other country.

The United States has long neglected to develop a comprehensive violence prevention strategy. There are more animal shelters in the United States than shelters for battered women. More legal gun dealers than gas stations, more murderers than in all the other industrial countries of the world combined. The United States is the only country in recorded history where children routinely kill children with no apparent motivation.

Few Americans realize that the unprecedented violence against African-American males is poisoning society as a whole. And most people still see violence as largely a criminal justice concern when, in fact, it is also a complicated public health, mental health, racial, economic, social and cultural condition.

Weisberg is a legal and political consultant. What he is describing, of course, is the context of actual violence in the United States, as opposed to the selective approach generally used by American politicians and the media, that is, visible, interpersonal street crime that affects the general public. Weisberg has enlarged the frame and scope of violence to include all types of violence, interpersonal and institutional.

The idea of escalating violence in the United States should not signify that the United States is alone in this issue. Headlines scream across Europe as crime and violence soar in France, Germany, England, and Italy—all across the European continent as well as the rest of the world. Weisberg has been able to bring to our attention the essence of what megacities around the world are facing—a tremendous rise in violence and violent activity.

Finally, escalating violence and crime are both a symptom and a
source of megacity insecurity. Institutional violence *by the state, war,*
civil war, ethnic strife, corporate violence, interpersonal violence *such*
as crime, violence against women and children, and intrapersonal
violence, *such as suicide or drug abuse, are growing. Violent crime*
has doubled in the last two decades and property crime tripled.
Violence and crime have become both internationalized and internal-
ized. Megacities become the major markets for the global drugs and
arms trade and the epicenters of domestic insecurity. Money launder-
ing from illicit drugs amounts to more than the gross national product
of three quarters of the world's economies. Consumer spending on
illicit drugs in the U.S. alone amounts to more than the gross domes-
tic product of more than 80 developing nations.[69]

Megacities are defined by Weisberg and the Security in
Megacities projects as the twenty-one cities across the globe with
populations of over ten million. He says we have come to understand
that *urban insecurity*, its conditions, causes and cures, are a major
context in which to understand the global movement of both capital
and people, and that the worldwide rising tide of violence is not
merely an American phenomenon. It is a world phenomenon and it
calls for systemic change in our approach to the human condition.

Reports from authorities on such cities state that the largest
cities of the world are becoming the epicenter of insecurity and conflict. The reasons they give for this, of course, is the escalating concentration of wealth, information, and people in megacities.
However, this movement has not included community as a way of
dealing with the human side of the equation, so therefore, the scale
in which these cities are built and developed does not lend itself to
behaving like villages or neighborhoods wherein people can have
relationships with each other. Because of the concentration of
wealth and poverty on the two extremes, a collision of values, of
relationships, and of security appears to be developing.

Various barriers do not allow for communication between
groups that are different. Instead, there is concentration on social
relationships almost completely with groups that are alike, thus
causing conflict, misunderstanding, inability to communicate, fear,
and fear of the unknown, as well as the desire to take from those
who do not have because they cannot afford to maintain themselves
in cities.

Experts like Weisberg see the growth of a global economy, the world-wide drug trade, and the critical role played by new technology as the culprits. People who are poor and without specific skills become surplus. They are not needed for the growth and development of this worldwide economy.

Janice Pearlman and the Mega-Cities Project, which she directs, are concentrating on ways to transfer knowledge between communities to revitalize the communities so that they can once again raise their children, make a living, and live without fear among their own people and others.

Weisberg has developed a metaphorical definition of the megacity phenomenon.

The megacity is, today, a metaphor for a global deconstructive process in which global markets replace local markets . . . institutional services or deprivation replaces family reliance, and self reliance; complex technology replaces traditional production systems and labor requirements; megacities depose nations as primary political and economic units; urban street war replaces battlefield combat; autistic violence usurps the social contract; crime supersedes the rule of law; and the informal economy parallels the formal economy. Thus there is an urgent need for a dynamic theory of megacity growth (and megacity security), within the global context, in order to find new strategies to nourish productive people, functional families, and political participation.[70]

Having posed the questions of the global deconstructive process, nations, states, and cities must still attempt to carry on while a cure is sought. In a speech given at the University of Illinois at Chicago in September 1995, Olivier DéGeorges discussed the growing problem of violence in France.

Revolutions have been part of the history of France. . . . Rioting has become, since the early '80s, a new expression of urban and social violence. Today, more than 32 neighborhoods in France are considered as "hypersensitive," they are the seeds of daily violence at a high level which often reveals itself by aggressions against police officers as well as a tendency to close a certain territory to outsiders and representatives of public authority. This . . . rejection of the outside world and creation of "extra-terrestrial areas" in which public power is not wel-

come strangely recalls from the Bronx to the favellas of Rio, a more global urban phenomenon: the appearance within our cities of new frontier lines that delineate not the rich from the less rich, but those who have work from those who do not even know what work and mainstream society is about. These neighborhoods have become 'supermarkets of drugs' in which various groups fight for hegemony. Some of the most spectacular riots in France in recent years have been started or fueled by drug dealers trying to preserve their territory.[71]

This should sound vaguely familiar; it is something that we hear, read, and have first-hand knowledge about in the United States. Generally, the media and politicians in our country pose these situations as if the rest of the world is a completely peaceful kingdom where there is no violence, no gunfire, no rioting. Here, we have the head of the major organization that works with towns and cities across the globe stating that in other parts of the world this is certainly not so, in fact, they parallel our own daily violence. In some ways it appears that it is at a much higher level, yet the hysteria is not, reportedly, quite as great as that in the United States. To again quote DéGeorges:

Apart from these 32 hypersensitive neighborhoods, the police report mentions for 1993, 105 high-risk neighborhoods in which daily violence takes the form of repeated aggressions against all the representatives of public institutions (schools, urban transport, firemen, police forces, social services), often under the form of very visible rejection (throwing of stones, graffiti, burning of private cars, etc.).

The Paris region concentrates a large proportion of each of these dysfunctioning neighborhoods, whatever the category, but apart from these urban and suburban centers, uncertainty and its corollary, insecurity is also present in more rural and remote urban centers. There, the forms of despair are different, and are oriented to oneself and to others or society in general: suicide, alcoholism, domestic violence, fights and car accidents. In these more rural neighborhoods, say the police reports, 'The experience of exclusion results in auto-depreciation and fatalism.'

The specificity of urban violence in France today is two-fold: On the one hand, the rise of 'civic offenses,' whether individual or collective, such as graffiti and destruction of public goods of a "recreational nature"; on the other hand, the formation of groups which identify themselves to some distinct element (music, etc.) and develop a sub-culture hostile to any form of authority. The recent French movie, The Hate, *which will be released in the United States, perfectly describes these mechanisms.*[72]

In the final analysis, what we are looking for, of course, are cures. But, from Europe, there comes the conclusion that there are no specific cures; that they, as we, are trying various kinds of projects, policies, and grassroots attempts to stem the tide of urban violence and trying to bring some kind of rational relationship back to people and the environments in which they live. It seems likely that this growing economic gap of disproportional scale relative to income, knowledge, skills, etc., is only going widen, and it is somewhere in that gap that the whole of civilization could be plunged if we do not begin immediately to find some way to create the context wherein public kinship and communication between people in society can take place.

DéGeorges does, however, offer some ideas based on the work of the many cities and towns throughout the world with which he has been associated. One is that there must be more city-to-city relationships irrespective of nation-states, and he outlines the following as ideas that should be followed up to find some cure to urban insecurity:

* Participation of inhabitants.
* Partnership and coordination of services.
* Decentralization and neighborhood democracy.
* Articulation with national regulations, services, and policies.
* Contracting between various levels of government for mutual, financial, logistic, and administrative support.
* Fight for education for all.
* Scholastic absenteeism and problems at school.
* Promotion of activities of and by young people.
* Integration of ethnic minorities.
* Local strategies for the reinsertion of delinquents and rehabilitation of victims.
* Collecting the right data and developing bridging programs with the police.
* Improving the physical urban environment.
* Fighting drug abuse.

Integrating the Margins

DéGeorges discusses an idea he calls, "integrating the margins." In effect, this particular idea was defined by DéGeorges as bringing the extremes into community and communication with the polis. Integrating the margins is, indeed, an applicable motto for all cities and towns across the world trying to remain civil today. This idea of integrating the margins carries with it the understanding of the social contract, which is a part of the idea of a civil government—a social contract that creates and binds the citizens of a commonwealth. It is, therefore, incumbent upon us that these ideas be brought to bear now upon this volatile situation. Without a clear-cut public policy, social policy, youth policy, and commitment by community as well as business and industry to integrating the margins into the entire makeup of society, we are doomed.

It is obvious that a new look at civic life and civil institutions is necessary, but this cannot take place unless there is a social contract which binds life to life, citizen to citizen, group to group, and above all, a civic compact which includes the economic institutions of the nation in the community and the world. The idea that global industries have no responsibility to the communities in which they live, in which they develop, and in which they have workers, and from which they take from the environment is morally inconsistent with our national values and our religious heritage. Whatever the relationship between capitalism and democracy, we need to clarify it, so we can plan for the future. Violence is more than street crime, the world over.

Fitting the Poor into the Economy

Herbert J. Ganz's article, "Fitting the Poor Into the Economy," appeared in the October 1995 edition of *Forum*. The opening statement is salient for this discussion:

> *The notion of the poor as too lazy or morally deficient to deserve assistance seems to be indestructible. Public policies limit poor people to substandard services and incomes below the subsistence level, and Congress and state legislatures are tightening up even on these misery allocations—holding those in the underclass responsible for their own sorry state. Indeed, labeling the poor as undeserving has lately become politically useful as a justification for the effort to eliminate much of*

*the anti-poverty safety net and permit tax cuts for the affluent people
who do most of the voting.*[73]

It is important to understand what Ganz has to say regarding
fitting the poor into the economy because, in fact, they do not fit
into the economy. This is undeniably one reason for the tremendous
violence in America's inner cities, and particularly with young urban
black men. The same can be said, however, across the globe, from
what we understand about cities and towns throughout Europe and
the rest of the world. The galloping global economy has preordained
a certain dislodging of particular kinds of laborers.

In 1970, in a book entitled, *Who Needs the Negro?*, Sidney M.
Wilhelm made a prediction that has come true, and that is with the
end of the agricultural economy and the beginning of the end of the
industrial economy, and the rise of the new economy of knowledge-
based and technological high skills, the African-American would be
in the unenviable position of having those who run the society ask
the question, "who needs the Negro?"

Wilhelm said that this would be the first time in American history that the American Negro would no longer be needed in the economic system whatsoever. However, African-Americans had not had
time to sit down, to study, to think about, and to understand the
coming consequences for their employment base. Frankly, they were
probably too much engaged in attempting simply to get simple civil
rights, dignity, and justice within the American system to understand that the economy that they were fighting to become a part of
and have access to was, in fact, quickly dying. Jeremy Rifkin, in *The
End Of Work*, quotes Wilhelm:

> *With the onset of automation, the Negro moves out of his historical
> state of oppression into one of uselessness. Increasingly, he is not so
> much economically exploited as he is irrelevant ... The dominant
> whites no longer need to exploit the black minority, as automation
> proceeds, it will be easier for the former to disregard the latter. In
> short, white America, by a more perfect application of mechanization
> and a vigorous alliance from automation disposes of the Negro.
> Consequently, the Negro transforms from an exploited labor force into
> an outcast.*[74]

This is true not only for the African-American unskilled, but is
true of all semi-skilled or unskilled labor around the world. But in

America, we are not asking what will happen to poor white people. It is as though they do not exist or a place will be made for them. With all of these facts in mind, and the global context set regarding violence, the larger issue here can be articulated. This issue is how to develop a *public idea* that will capture the imagination, the will, and the power of individuals acting together to change this system of social destruction. It is certainly true that in America, a large and significant portion of crime and violence can be related to African-American men, but this is not the whole picture.

It is also true that there is an escalating rise in violence throughout the United States among all categories of youth, including blacks, Hispanics, whites and others. If we could see even that in holistic terms, then we could go on to develop some kind of national strategies. The latest report on youth crime and its significant rise is quoted below:

The increase in the juvenile arrest rate for violent crimes began in the late 1980's

During the period from 1973 through 1988 the number of juvenile arrests for a Violent Crime Index offense (murder and nonnegligent manslaughter, forcible rape, robbery, and aggravated assault) varied with the changing size of the juvenile population. However, in 1989, the juvenile violent crime arrest rate broke out of this historic range.

The years between 1988 and 1991 saw a 38 percent increase in the rate of juvenile arrests for violent crimes. The rate of increase then diminished, with the juvenile arrest rate increasing little between 1991 and 1992. This rapid growth over a relatively short period moved the juvenile arrest rate for violent crime in 1992 far above any year since the mid-1960's, the earliest time period for which comparable statistics are available.

The juvenile violent crime arrest rate increased substantially in all racial groups in recent years

In 1983 the violent crime arrest rate for black youth was nearly 7 times the white rate. Between 1983 and 1992 the white arrest rate increased more than the black arrest rate increased (82 percent vs. 43 percent). As a result, in 1992 the rate of violent crime arrests for black youth was about 5 times the white rate.

Over the 10-year period from 1983 through 1992, the violent crime arrest rate for youth of other races increased 42 percent, nearly equal to the increase in the black rate.[75]

With this in mind, we must now create a *public idea* that calls for understanding these issues. Grassroots democracy and the polis are concepts developed in this report that can serve as key public ideas. To integrate the margins will require developing public kinship, this common culture that we must strive for so that we bring communication and vision to people in communities, people in government, and people in industry.

In fact, Robert Putnam states very clearly that what makes democracy work is people in relationships—grassroots democracy. America, then, can become the model of putting that grassroots democratic process into place. Putnam's research made the following discovery relative to civic engagement:

Now we draw a map of Italy in 1993 according to wealth. We will find that communities with many choral societies are also more advanced economically. I originally thought that these fortunate communities have more choral societies because they were wealthy. After all, I thought, poor peasants didn't have time or energy to spend singing. But if we look closely at the historical record, it becomes clear that I had it exactly wrong. Communities don't have choral societies because they are wealthy; they are wealthy because they have choral societies—or more precisely, the traditions of engagement, trust and reciprocity that choral societies symbolize.

Of two equally poor Italian regions a century ago, both very backward, but one with more civic engagement and the other with a hierarchical structure, the one with more choral societies and soccer clubs has grown steadily wealthier. The more civic region has prospered because the trust and reciprocity are woven into its social fabric ages ago. None of this would appear in standard economic textbooks, of course, but our evidence suggests that wealth is the consequence, not the cause of a healthy community.[76]

Putnam is illuminating the idea that getting people to work together and play together in productive group activities builds community economic success.It may well be that the way to outwit the rising tide of youth violence and violence in general in a global context is to reinvigorate the idea of individuals in communities engaging in civic acts with each other. It is then possible that we can talk about how to affect the economies of communities. These kinds of public ideas must be brought out in our public dialogue. They are much more important in the United States than building jails and scapegoating. We must, then, "integrate the margins," thus invigorating the public ideas of grassroots democracy and civic re-engagement.

Youth violence does not seem to be subsiding even though crime, in general, is decreasing in the United States. Communities throughout the nation feel extremely insecure. Part of this, of course, is that, economically, these are transitional times that we live in. Also, we appear to be considering a political Contract with America as opposed to a social contact between individuals and groups in this society. Individuals and groups in our society, more than ever, need to be closer together because of the traumatic experiences of many fellow citizens.

Alcoholism, suicide, unwanted pregnancies, sexually transmitted diseases, and crime all are climbing among youth populations around the world. These are signs that there is a need for understanding of the issues and comprehensive planning for youth to successfully come into their own as contributing individuals in the society. They must have a chance to envision a future. This chance is the best gift that this generation can give its offspring.

The society of the present is creating the society of the future without really having models to rely on. Consequently, young people will need to have personal inner reserves that may not have been developed. In fact, they probably have not been developed by many adults. Young people will have to be independent moral agents in a way that few generations of young people have been called to be before in our history. Perhaps they will be that group that can face this daunting task as no other generation has. The task of creating those public ideas and new visions belongs to us. We will need to refocus our sights on what violence is, how we create community, and what the consequences are if we fail.

REPAIRERS OF THE BREACH, RESTORERS OF THE STREETS TO DWELL IN:
An Integrated Plan of Action

*I*N the beginning of 1995, Ambassador Andrew Young delivered a nationally televised sermon on the *Hour of Power*, from the pulpit of the Crystal Cathedral, Reverend Robert Schuller's church in California. Ambassador Young found his text in the Book of Isaiah (Chapter 58:9–12):

> *Then you shall call, and the Lord will answer; you shall cry, and He will say, Here I am. If you take away from the midst of you the yoke, the pointing of the finger, and speaking wickedness, if you pour yourself out for the hungry and satisfy the desire of the afflicted, then shall your light rise in the darkness and your gloom be as the noonday. And the Lord will guide you continually and satisfy your desire with good things, . . . you shall be like a watered garden, like a spring of water whose waters fail not. And your ancient ruins shall be rebuilt; you shall raise up the foundations of many generations; you shall be called the repairer of the breach, the restorer of streets to dwell in. (RSV)*

This message was so powerful because it said in several ways that the only way to reestablish community is to become a repairer of the breach, a restorer of safe streets to dwell in. It is the underpinning of the holistic approach to helping boys who are in trouble move away from trouble, to engaging their families, to building citi-

170

zens, and thus, to raising the foundations of many generations of persons of good will.

Young stressed in his sermon that we have to begin anew, and begin first with our children to reestablish with them the priorities in life, both material and physical. Then, above all things, it will take the spiritual to repair this rupture.

Throughout this entire process, one of the most strongly felt emotions from all the grantees, from the participants at all the meetings, and from the members of the Task Force, was a tremendous reservoir of deep spiritual feeling. There has not been a gathering in which prayers have not been offered and praise has not been sung. At every meeting people have been in accord and blessed their God. Such is the strength of this spiritual revival within the individuals who are coming forth to begin to repair the breach.

But these repairers of the breach can not work alone, for it is obvious that to repair the breach within the present political society, to reestablish civil life, and to reconstruct civic institutions that will carry on that life, government and the economic system must also play a part. It may seem to some that public policy would rely primarily upon a certain sense of reason and political practicality, but such is not the case.

J. W. Gough, of Oxford University, commenting on John Locke's *Second Treatise of Government* and *a Letter Concerning Toleration* says:

> *What seems to me to the lasting value of Locke, is his insistence on the responsibility of the State to the community—ultimately its responsibility for the welfare of the community. This principle is now commonly admitted, and we have elaborated the political mechanism by which responsibility is made effective. This, rather than consent, is the real point of election and representation.*[77]

It appears to be Locke's view that the governed, having created the government through their consent, have a right to make certain claims upon that government; and that both the governed and the government have duties and responsibilities to sift and sort how conflicting claims are to be adjudicated.

Thus, the concept of leadership espoused by James MacGregor Burns, with its central emphasis on how moral, social, and political order is shaped through the interaction of leadership and conflict, is of extreme importance at this time because public policy seems to vacillate and change at warp speed. However, the context of that change should not be always at the whim of any group that takes power.

Emerson states, "The vice of our leading parties in this country, which may be cited as a fair specimen of these societies of opinion, is that they do not plant themselves on the deep and necessary grounds to which they are respectively entitled, but lash themselves to fury in the caring of some local and momentary measure, no wise useful to the Commonwealth."[78]

That indictment is a stinging one, and is absolutely appropriate for today. Locke states, "The Commonwealth seems to me to be a society of men constructed only for the procuring, preserving, and advancing their own civil interests. Civil interests, I call life, liberty, health, and indolency of body, and the possession of outward things such as money, land, houses, furniture, and the like." In essence, he establishes the bond of the Commonwealth with its people and what it must procure. In a most interesting way, it boils down to life, liberty, and the pursuit of happiness; and how one is to find ways to do that.

Public policy, then, in the United States has to work within these concepts. James O'Toole places the moving public policy pendulum between certain goals. He states that

> we must begin with what George Will calls the four "great themes of political argument." My basic contention is that there are four such themes or dreams: liberty, equality, efficiency and community. The countless competing views of the good society, propounded over the millennium and the position staked out on most issues being debated today in Washington and local governments, can be sorted into these four dreams.[79]

These four themes must be the centerpiece of our public discourse regarding public policy. These themes (or dreams) undergird the process that would aid the repairers of the breach in American communities to facilitate development and healthy growth within American society. As Booker T. Washington admonished the African-American many years ago, "It must be remembered that no individual or race can contribute to the solution of any general problem until he has first worked out his own peculiar problem."[80] This becomes the public policy dimension that must be worked out by African-Americans. They must first go to the grassroots level in urban communities. Each community can work out its own scenario. This is not to say that we are not dealing with a universal problem, or a societal problem, or a national problem; but in the final analysis, it is a personal, ethnic problem that must be dealt with.

The thinkers and prophets of the African-American race, intellectual, political, and social, have enumerated the values that are necessary. Now the next tier of this work must be done. As each generation moves higher and higher we are left with what is called the underclass to reorient. All the recommendations point to the fact that this can and must be done.

Reconstructing civil society and civic life within these communities becomes an important part of public policy, and it is the part that African-Americans must play with the aid and assistance of institutions such as foundations and businesses. All levels of state and local government are struggling to address the continuing social disintegration as part and parcel of this issue. A new public policy strategy will go a long way to drawing out and sharing lessons that have been learned as to how to recreate civil life. In the work of the National Task Force on African-American Men and Boys, the leadership dimension is a critical link between policy and program initiative.

By attention to leadership development the tone is set for both government and philanthropy to recognize that there must be strong emphasis on the development of those individuals who appear to be among the solid creative anchors in their communities, creating what Michael Pertschuk calls "Citizen Leadership." Thus, investment in individuals who can make a difference will be a vital and critical need in public policy development in our nation's urban communities. Government must enhance the work of these solid citizens who can bring change at the local level.

Politicians

The National Caucus of Black State Legislators, comprised of all the nation's black state legislators, has begun to develop State Commissions as an organized response to this crisis. The Ohio Commission on African-American Men, the first to be developed, is the prototype for their action. The idea is to promote successful projects within states, with each state being able to replicate those projects it deems appropriate and necessary for its situation. Legislators would, through law and policy options, convert successful ideas into public programs and statewide initiatives where feasible. Senator Frank Bowen, a member of the task force, is the originator of this unique policy-program initiative. These Commissions are working examples of politicians and communities working together.

Foundations

There are at least four areas where public policy and grantmaking meet on this national issue: (1) By facilitating community leadership, new leaders are brought to the fore to voice the needs of the group in crisis; (2) by forming a cooperative group, community leaders will be able to further develop collaborative techniques within communities and in the public dialogue; (3) by creating joint approaches with government, the private sector, and foundations, issues can be discussed through a combined approach that would define how to strengthen communities and their leadership, and; (4) by providing public officials with the best practices and lessons learned from successful projects, these can be replicated.

Public Policy for the Common Good: A Civic Compact

There needs to be a greater and greater emphasis on local family policy or neighborhood policy that would forge a link between the home, the school, the church, and the business community, knowing full well that none of these can stand alone. This emphasis then points public policy toward how to integrate and utilize the vast and existing services of all governments across the nation to create partnerships for liveable metropolitan areas—improving the human condition in America.

It is apparent that this new approach to public policy may take some of the sting out of the competing and conflicting political positions regarding liberty, equality, efficiency, and community. Trade-offs between them will not provide the nation with the kind of population that will make it both competitive and stable in the coming years. It is apparent, then, that a new civic compact, drawn between the governed and those who govern, will be essential over the coming years, but no longer will politicians of any stripe or race be able to use the issue of race as a defining factor in deciding whether people should ask for liberty, equality, efficiency, or whatever. The new civic compact must be based on a more holistic approach of what is best for the society. It must answer how we create a whole society that looks at the human condition, and how citizens take part in discussion with the government that they have created. The new civic compact must be created by citizens and their representatives, acting for the citizens and not themselves.

The Task Force obviously hopes that this new way of looking at how to bring violence under control, to be the repairers of the breach and the restorers of the streets, has with it a spiritual, a practical, and a political element, all of which must work together if we are to create a better society for these boys and their families, as well as the entire nation.

This is not just an African-American problem, but this is an American problem as well, as it is a national and international problem that calls for the reengagement of young people, for a reduction of violence, and for the uplifting of certain virtues and values, which would lead to a more sane approach to life on this planet.

The new civic compact would, then, be one more tool within the public policy arena that politicians could use to bring about respect and understanding between groups as opposed to the continual inflaming of individuals to distrust, dislike, and seek revenge upon others.

This compact would also have to include the American media. In the eyes of many observers, the media are among the key contributors to the destabilization, not only of these communities, but of the nation at large.

Jay Rosen of New York University, the director of Public Life and the Press, states in an article published for the Kettering Foundation that:

> Good journalism requires more than good journalists—more even than enlightened ownership, First Amendment protections, and a strong economic base. For without an engaged and concerned public, even the most public-minded press cannot do its job. Thus the involvement of people in the affairs of their community, their interest in political discussion, their willingness to abandon a spectator's role and behave as citizens—all form the civic capital on which the enterprise of the press is built. To live off that capital without trying to replenish it is a dangerous course for journalists to follow; but this is precisely the predicament of the American press today. It addresses a "public" it does little to help create.[81]

Civic culture can be strengthened by creating a new approach that does not start with conflict and blame. These factors do not make for the strengthening of community bonds and civic culture.

Public policy, then, must become aligned with the repairers of the breach and the restorers of streets. It is the work of the politician and of the citizenry. It must not, simply, boil down to competing themes, but common themes of public kinship.

The Fourth Sector

The work of the African-American Men and Boys initiative and the National Task Force on African-American Men and Boys can lead to the creation of a fourth sector in the African-American community.

Three sectors are already well defined and established—educational, religious, and civil rights/political. The missing sector is that of the civic, social, and cultural. There are already many strong and active organizations in these areas. But their voices have not yet been brought together. In order for the numerous recommendations of the Task Force to be successfully implemented, there must be a strong, robust network of community civic, social, and cultural organizations working together. The involvement of this fourth sector is essential if the Integrated Plan of Action is to succeed.

The loss of a social center in some neighborhoods and communities requires that our civic, social, cultural, and religious organizations begin immediately to study their individual areas, to plan from the local to the national, to combine their efforts to accomplish programs, to cooperate in long-range planning, and to develop an organized companionship working toward the goal of restoring the economic and social future of the community.

Agenda building and planning must be based on the goals, missions, and aspirations of those affected. If these organizations can become a working network, this would give rise to a further national dialogue, adding voices to the existing civil rights organizations. The dialogue would focus on building bridges and would be based on a sense of community mission.

Civic, social, cultural, and religious organizations can be a new voice of grassroots democracy, experience, and resolve, working together to solve problems. The unity and strength developed by these organizations of the fourth sector can be a powerful tool for organizing and leveraging change in the coming decade.

Bringing together this sector would enlist a large cadre of resourceful citizens and established institutions. This would add muscle to the existing leadership and organizations working to improve conditions in our communities.

An Integrated Plan of Action

To bring about this new civic engagement at the grassroots level to help the nation's poor citizens who are troubled, who are in violent situations, who may commit crimes, and who have often neglected their responsibilities, will require a unity among all Americans, but specifically, at its beginning, among Americans of African descent.

Calls for unity among African-Americans are as annual as daffodils in spring. Unity calls are made every year from one segment or another of the race. Without these annual rites we might be unsure as to what our leadership is doing. These calls are important because they are a public reaffirmation of desire and commitment.

It is clear, however, that the time has come when black people in the United States must develop a new voice, a voice that states in clear, unfettered tones the progress of this New World people. These are people that James Baldwin applauds as having created a history of accomplishment known the world over in just three hundred years and whom Lorraine Hansberry describes as a classical people. These people must decide not if they can or will unify or if they will survive, but for what purpose, what goals, what mission they will, once again, gather around. They will speak of survival not in terms of survival "at any cost," but in relation to the quality of that survival—which makes mere survival a non-issue. These people will consider the potential good that they and their future generations will bring to bear on the American common culture.

The social center of American common life is that core of values, ethics, and moral principles that has been the "North Star" of African-Americans since before America was America. If we acknowledge that this center is deteriorating, then we recognize that this is due to rapid changes in society, less economic opportunity, a loss of values, and loss of respect for self and community, spurred by advancing technology. For this reason, entry into the next century will be a perilous journey for us all. Yet, we must face the fact that many segments of our society may be expendable because they were never allowed to become participants in our national life and its supporting economy. Consequently, they will have no marketable skills and they will be adrift in a society which has lost sight of its own historic social center. These will be dangerous times. The course of the voyage between these transitional years into the years 2000, 2020, and 2050 is now quite unpredictable.

It is within this context that we must raise calls of unity. The question becomes: How can black Americans restore the social center of their own people and develop a substantive unified voice which facilitates entry into the next century?

A Classical Approach

As a classical people, black Americans must know that unity by its very nature and definition in the American body politic cannot be racially circumscribed. It must be inclusive. Louis Lomax is quoted as saying, "If the Russians dropped a bomb on Manhattan, it would blow Harlem to Hell." This is a political and social reality. We must, however, be pragmatic enough to know that unity within our own group must be tackled first if progress toward national unity is to be addressed.

Frederick Douglass, addressing this issue in *The Nation's Problem,* wrote the following:

> *A nation within a nation is an anomaly. There can be but one American nation under the American government, and we [black Americans] are Americans. . . . We cannot afford to draw the color lines in politics, trades, education, manners, religion, fashion or civilization. Especially, we cannot afford to draw the color line in politics.*
>
> *No folly could be greater. A party acting upon that basis would be not merely a misfortune but a dire calamity to our people. The rule of the majority is the fundamental principle of the American government and it may be safely affirmed that the American people will never permit, tolerate or submit to the success of any political devise or strategy calculated to circumvent and divert . . . this principle.*[82]

As one of our nation's preeminent political philosophers, Douglass understood the fundamental elements required for unity in our community and in America, and he did not see them as being mutually exclusive.

In this classic sense, the task before us is twofold. First, black Americans must get their house in order (restoring their social center) and second, black Americans must get America together by being that moral wedge that informs the collective conscience of the nation.

The Social Center

But how do we do this? How do we maintain and improve the social center? And how does a group become the moral wedge?

These questions require that black Americans face up to the fact of the rapid deterioration of our physical and social life and that we come together to solve the problems. This is pivotal and it is a difficult task. Again, we quote Douglass.

In pointing out errors and mistakes common among ourselves, I shall run the risk of incurring displeasure; for no people with whom I am acquainted are less tolerant of criticism than ourselves, especially from one of our own number. We have been so long in the habit of tracing our failures and misfortunes to the views and acts of others that we seem, in some measure, to have lost the talent and disposition of seeing our own faults, or of seeing ourselves as others see us. And yet no man can do a better service to another man than to correct his mistakes, point out his hurtful errors, show him the path of truth, duty and safety. [83]

A comprehensive study of our progress, problems, and our possibilities can come from a hard and critical look at ourselves. Such an examination would necessarily focus on "babies with babies"; the rapid increase of female-headed households; the rise in the number of battered and abused children; the alarming increase in suicide rates among our youth; the well-documented, widespread abuse of drugs; and the frightening status of the unemployed in our communities whose numbers grow daily. These are some of the alarming facts of our national life. They will not go away of their own accord and are but a reflection of graver problems that lie ahead. These are the first signs of an expendable group in a changing economy; an economy preparing for a high-technology and low-manpower future. What will become of these people? Who needs them? These are but two of the questions that must be answered.

Our community has initiated a plethora of social programs, some good, some not so good. Most were a part of the poverty politics of the 1960s and the 1970s. These programs and politics focused national black leadership toward sociopolitical ends.

The relationship of programs relative to affirmative action and the advance of the black middle class is apparent. One is hard pressed to say the same for the outcomes of many social programs and the underclass. The reality today, however, is that a weak social community cannot sustain the strong, sophisticated political activism that is needed. Politics will require a lot more than marching. We must have the collective strengths of our people in an orchestrated chorus of voices to articulate change throughout the established institutions of our nation.

The loss of the social center in our neighborhoods, towns, and cities requires that our civic, social, religious, and cultural organizations begin immediately to plan from the local to the national level, to jointly study their individual areas, to combine their efforts in programming, to cooperate in long-range planning, and to develop a sense of organized companionship toward the goal of restoring our future in social and economic terms.

Some steps have already been made in this direction. As reported in the black press, the nation's largest black Greek organizations have begun just such cooperative planning. Others must follow their lead. Then, combining our total strength and manpower, our people and our nation can be helped.

The Moral Wedge

By challenging our civic, social, religious, and cultural organizations to take our future in hand and work together to solve our problems, we create a new voice; a voice of freedom, experience, and stable resolve. It is not impossible to achieve this kind of unity—and to go beyond that to see our unity as the moral wedge in the coming decade. Dr. Martin Luther King, Jr., was able to pull together the most effective proof of racial and national unity within one broad political-social movement. As a minister, he understood the deeply held spiritual and social beliefs of his people and he used this to galvanize the many disparate parts into a political unit that smashed age-old social and political barriers.

Leadership today grapples with ideas of black agendas and black plans but nationally syndicated columnist William Raspberry asked in his June 10, 1983, column, "What is the Black Agenda?" No one honestly seems to have the slightest idea. He went on to wonder if one really exists.

Agenda-building and planning must take place in and around some general discussion of the goals, the missions, and the aspirations of those affected. If our civic, social, religious, and cultural organizations can develop themselves into a working network, they will add their voices to our existing civil rights organizations. The dialogue would focus on the bridges that must be built over this national transitional sea; a dialogue based on the studies and the sense of community mission of these organizations.

This national dialogue must bring to the fore that large cadre of resourceful people and solid institutions in our towns and cities to add muscle to our leadership and to our national development. This would be a dialogue between equal independent groups and organizations talking about the issues which concern everyone. Here, the black press could play a crucial role in fostering the dialogue and exporting it into the larger public arena.

This kind of leadership fosters the common good and establishes a style that does not come to the nation as a beggar at the gate or as a "spoilsport" but as a people of prophetic vision.

A Harmonious Design

A national conversation on race has been proposed, but this report is most assuredly addressed to African-Americans, and an organized approach is needed to secure their future in this nation.

The dictionary defines unity as a complex union of related parts or an arrangement of parts that will produce a single harmonious design. Unity on the part of black Americans can probably best be accomplished by a new national dialogue, sparked and carried on by the combined and organized civic, social, religious, and cultural voices that seek to recreate the social center while at the same time embodying the force of a prophetic moral wedge.

National Organizational Meeting

Following the theme of the report, a think tank/work group will implement a national organized meeting. This will follow up on the internal dialogue within the African-American community. This will begin the development of an organized civic, social, religious, and cultural sector within the African-American community to support and implement Project 2000 and the Generation Plan. This new civic sector could be a key to stabilizing families and communities that are near collapse. It would add a new voice to the arena of public opinion. Many such groups, some 300 to 400, currently act in concert with each other, but this would be the first time they would be asked to organize nationally to accomplish the specific goal of repairing the social breach and restoring safe streets in communities

Repairing the Breach

What follows is a proposal for a sequential program for the development of a network of civic, social, religious, and cultural organizations (the fourth sector), and the black press and those engaged in

civic journalism, to create unity in the African-American community, to continue the work of the internal dialogue and support implementation of the Task Force action plan outlined below. This will be
the foundation for creating polis, public kinship, and good civic stories. This would be the first operational program in the national
work group. The program as proposed would be a pilot demonstra-
tion to span approximately four years: one year in planning and
preparation and three years in operation.

The intent is to enlist and motivate the national and local leadership of major organizations to work cooperatively to sponsor local
programs aimed at developing a solid internal dialogue process at the
neighborhood level through spiritual and ethical restoration, using
the model established by the Task Force. Success would be measured
by its adoption and elaboration on an ever-widening scale. This program would be one of the first operational programs of the reconstituted think tank/work group. A Wingspread Conference to initiate
the development of this civic sector has been proposed.

The work would occur in three phases. These are outlined here
and are covered in more detail below.

Phase I involves selection and recruitment of interested national civic, social, religious, and cultural organization leaders to discuss,
define, refine, and elaborate these concepts: (1) unity, (2) civic dialogue, (3) the social center, (4) the moral wedge, (5) polis, (6) parallel
economy, (7) public kinship, (8) integrating the margins, (9) common
good, and (10) civic story telling. As this project is conceived, the
black press is a critical element in two major aspects: (1) as contributors to the dialogue because they know their communities, and (2) as
interpreters and communicators of the dialogue to their readership.

Heads of selected major organizations involved in educational,
political, religious, civic, social, business, and professional activities,
along with members of the NNPA, would be invited to participate in
a workshop to lay the framework for reconstructing the social center
of our neighborhoods, towns, and cities.

This first workshop should propose two major programs to be
implemented through the collaboration and cooperation of all the
organizations. Examples might be a program both symbolic and
artistic using drama and pageantry to develop spirit and focus among
the African-American people and their neighbors. The second program might be educational using the broad theme, "The World We
Live In" developed through pamphlets, books, exhibitions, essays,
lectures, and other activities designed for the entire family. The pro-

gram would be designed to actively involve participants in the study of black Americans and their place in American culture and in world history, linking our glorious past to the struggle for a greater future in the United States and the world. The third program might develop the Technology Centers as proposed in this National Task Force Report.

Local pilot programs would be supported by contributions of the various cooperating organizations over a three-year period and through funds obtained by the Task Force in cooperation with the nation's philanthropic community.

A second workshop would include a broader range of officials of major black organizations and institutions to develop a national network, create procedures for implementation, and identify target cities and target populations within those cities. This workshop should be held at a conference site in late spring, 1997.

The second phase is the implementation phase. All committed and interested group representatives and individuals will be invited to meet in conference to be held at a historically black college in October-November, 1997. This phase would focus on these matters: (1) develop a communications network; (2) define programs; (3) select cities; (4) recognize organizations and their key program personnel, endorsers, and sponsors; (5) establish a reporting and monitoring system; (6) prepare materials; (7) formally announce the program throughout the media; (8) conduct publicity, convene the conference; and (9) prepare and disseminate the report of the conference.

The third phase involves all of the activities of Phases I and II as well as publication of a periodic newsletter to provide the communications link between projects—giving news, progress reports, recognition of outstanding achievements, publicity and promotion, interchange about programs, and acknowledgment of sponsors and endorsers. The fourth sector should be established by this time. This end of this phase would coincide with the conclusion of Project 2000.

Scope of Work and Time Frame

Phase I covers the period September 1996 through August 1997 and involves the following activities:

- communications with appropriate organizations and individuals;
- recruitment of participating organizations;
- conference planning;

Phase II covers the period September 1997 through August 1998 and involves the following activities:

- conference planning;
- communication with potential participants;
- finalizing commitments;
- preparation of materials;
- developing communication network;
- publicity;
- convening the conference;
- preparation and dissemination of conference report.

Phase III covers the period from September 1998 through September 1999 and involves all of the activities of Phases I and II as well as publication and dissemination of a periodic newsletter providing the communication link between projects for progress reports of activities, recognition of outstanding achievement, programmatic interchange, publicity, promotion, and acknowledgment of sponsors and endorsers. The end of Phase III coincides with the end of Project 2000.

Project 2000

Project 2000 is the first five years of the Generation Plan—from summer 1996 to 2000. During this period items listed in the Integrated Plan of Action (pages 186–191) will be accomplished. This work will be implemented by the reconstituted National Task Force as the "Center for American Futures."

The Task Force has provided a set of recommendations based on themes. These can lead to a set of tools which could be used to restructure our frame of reference and our various mental models. Then we can be ready for further dialogue—a dialogue that could finally lead us to an open conversation within our groups and within our nation—regarding not just the issue of violence and African-American men and boys but the larger issue of which violence as a symptom. When we can agree that all of us are individual moral agents, and responsible for our own actions in this democracy, then a complete systems change will have occurred, and we will have been successful in creating the framework in which long-term sustained approaches to bringing all Americans into this democracy can be accomplished.

The Generation Plan

The Generation Plan is an attempt to specify steps that need to be taken over the next twenty years to secure the future of boys who are in trouble (pages 192–194). The plan is a "template," not a mandate. (When you read the names of implementors, these are merely suggestions, as these people have not been contacted to determine their availability or desire to implement.) The idea is to create discussion around the future development of a plan of action that can be agreed to and monitored.

> *Just when I thought I was lost, my dungeon shook and my chains fell off.*
>
> (Unknown African-American bard)

Task Force Recommenda-tions	Strategies	Implementation	Target Location	Time Line
Establish a Foundation and/or Trust Fund	A. Develop mission statement for a 501(c)(3).	Dr. Bobby Austin Peggy Cooper Cafritz		Jan. 1996
	B. Establish a 501(c)(3): American Institute on Race and Economics.	Kellogg Foundation Dr. Bobby Austin Robert Harris Robert Watson	Washington, DC	Feb.–Mar. 1996
Establish a National Think Tank	A. As a component of the newly established founda-tion, identify a steering/ planning committee.	Honorable Andrew Young Dr. Bobby Austin Dr. Georgia Sorenson Peggy Cooper Cafritz		April 1996
	B. Collaborate with Fisk University, other HBCUs, and the community college system.			June 1996
	C. Collaborate for purposes of analysis of similar entities: Joint Center for Political Studies; The Southern Center; etc.			
	D. Host a national town meet-ing with HBCUs serving as host sites	Honorable Andrew Young Dr. Carolyn Pegram		Sep. 1996
Facilitate a National Convers-ation on Race Relations	A. Revive the Race Relations Institute at Fisk University.	President of Fisk Dr. Paul DuBois	Fisk University - Race Relations Institute	1997
	B. Host community/local town meeting to "frame" the issues.	Dr. Bobby Austin Dr. Paul DuBois Congress of National Black Churches	Selected Kellogg AA Men and Boys Grantees' loca-tions	
	C. Develop six (6) working booklets on concepts tar-geting family, church, and community.	Kellogg, Closeup, and Kettering Foundations		
	D. Host a national town meet-ing via satellite as a kick-off event.	CRP, Inc.	HBCU campuses and majority uni-versities same as host sites	Nov. 1997

GRASSROOTS CIVIC LEADERSHIP

The systematic study of skills needed to mobilize, organize (economically, culturally, and politically), develop, and inspire those who will perform from positions of leadership in their communities.

Task Force Recommendations	Strategies	Implementation	Target Location	Time Line
#1 Training	Nationwide training for persons desiring to work as grassroots leaders in their communities, focusing on cultural and spiritual leadership.		Louisville, KY Milwaukee, WI Lawrence, KS Boston, MA Nashville, TN Houston, TX	1997– 2020
#2 Fellowship Program – 2 years	A. Fund national competitive fellowships for grassroots democracy leadership development.		Nationwide	1998– 2020
	B. Establish a National Leadership Institute of AA leaders with the purpose of increasing the number of young black men prepared to take leadership positions in business, civic, and political arenas.	A function of the new trust fund/foundation	Washington, DC	2000– 2026
#6A Learning Plan	Development of learning plans, modeled after the Kellogg design, by grassroots leadership fellows.		N/A	1998– 2026
#6B Journaling	A. Incorporate journaling as a component of the "learning plan" process.	N/A		1998– 2026
	B. Employ grassroots civic leaders to assist in the development of the learning plan and assist in monitoring the plans.	Select Civic leaders based on the location of the fellows	Match according to location of fellows	1998– 2026
#7 Entrepreneurship Economic Development	Establish a national, international, and regional advisory group that will work to establish an economic infrastructure in AA communities.	Function of the new Trust Fund foundation and select Task Force members	Four geographical regions: Southern; Eastern; Midwestern; Southwestern/ Western Regions	1996– 1997

Task Force Recommenda-tions	Strategies	Implementation	Target Location	Time Line
#10 National Summit on "Images of AA Men and Boys"	Host a summit on the topic inviting national media giants and counterparts regionally with the purpose of effecting change in media portrayal of AA males.	Kellogg Foundation and Corporation for Public Broadcasting	National/Media	1996–2000
#11 National Summit meeting of CEOs of major corporations	Host a summit inviting at least 200 CEOs of major corpora-tions for the purpose of devel-oping a plan for encouraging the development of entrepre-neurship opportunities among AA males.	Kellogg Foundation and select Steering Committee of CEOs	CEOs of major corporations; location to be identified through the Steering Committee	1997
#3 Center of Excellence	Establish 5 centers of excel-lence: 3 in urban areas and 2 in rural areas for the purpose of training for democratic effectiveness, providing access to education and employment systems, and racial harmony.	Kellogg Foundation with support of HBCUs and National organiza-tions (i.e., fraterni-ties, sororities, Masons, etc.)		
	Stage 1 Research and Development			1996–1997 (2 yrs.)
	Stage 2 Start-up			1998–2001 (3 yrs.)
	Stage 3 Early Growth			2002 -2006 (5 yrs.)
	Rapid Growth			2007–2016 (10 yrs.)
	Mature Organization			2017–2020 (3 yrs.)

Task Force Recommendations	Strategies	Implementation	Target Location	Time Line
#1 Establish a national center to coordinate and disseminate information about current positive programs and activities that exist		Dr. Bobby Austin Dr. Paul Dubois Center for Living Democracy	Kellogg AA project grantees	1996– 2000
#2 Establish a National Black Film Institute	Training and education should be the goals of this Institute.	Michael Schultz Selected Members of the Task Force	TBD	1997– 1998
#3 Development and implementation of a traveling Institute for African-American Males, an "Information on Wheels" program	This traveling Information Institute should also encourage reading and writing by African-American males about their current and historical experiences in America.	African-American Museum Association	Nationwide, but start with Kellogg AA project grantee communities	2000– 2010
#4 International Fellowship Summit for Black men. This summit should be held in the United States, but coordinated by Black men throughout the world. (See Grassroots Civic Leadership Recommendations 2B and 10.)	Unity; Economic Development; Jobs; Male/Female partnerships (at entry level); Strategies to strengthen family and community life, i.e., fathering, mothering, and mentoring; Spending money in black communities	A function of the new foundation	National; host city to be one of the Kellogg AA male project locations	1997– 1998

Task Force Recommendations	Strategies	Implementation	Target Location	Time Line
#7 Technology – Learning Centers (the teaching and learning strategies for the development of AA males and youth)	Establishment of technology learning centers as ancillary components to Kellogg- funded projects for AA men/boys focusing on values development, decision-making/ responsibility, self-identity, race relations, economic self-sufficiency, and mentoring.	Timothy Jenkins and Association Center for Living Democracy CRP, Inc.	Kellogg AA males project grantees Start-up in 5 cities	Planning Development 1996 June 1996
	Sharing/exchanging of ideas by each of the local sites in a group setting.	Hull House		Aug. 1996
	Development and distribution of success stories for the media.	Center for Living Democracy		Sep. 1996
	Ongoing evaluation of the project. Add 5 additional Kellogg-funded projects.			Oct.–Dec. 1996
	Development and distribution of success stories. Policies for the media.	Cluster Evaluation Team		Nov.–Dec. 1996–1999
	Invite national organizations to sponsor learning centers.	Newly organized Task Force Center "think tank"	Organizations represented on the Kellogg AA Men and Boys Task Force (i.e., Masons, Elks, fraternities, etc.)	Jan. 1997
	Collaborative Planning			Feb.–May 1997
	Kickoff of new learning centers sponsored by national organizations.			June 1997
	Development and distribution of media stories.	Center for Living Democracy		June 1997

CIVIC DIALOGUE (continued)

Task Force Recommendations	Strategies	Implementation	Target Location	Time Line
#7 (con't)	Sharing/exchanging of ideas by all learning centers (Kellogg grantees and national organizations).	CRP, Inc.		Aug. 1997
	Distribution of media stories.	Center for Living Democracy		Aug.–Sep. 1997
	Repeat the incremental addition of new learning centers, the planning process, start-up, etc.			1998–2000

RESTORING COMMUNITY

Task Force Recommendations	Strategies	Implementation	Target Location	Time Line
#1 Public Awareness of Successful Programs	Creation of an Information Resource Center (IRC) that would serve as a central clearing house of on-line information and database access; facilitate computer skills training; an on-line access; access to social services.	The Center for Living Democracy and National Trust for the Development of AA Men; National Association of African-American Men	Kellogg AA Project Grantees	1997
			National Organizations associated with Civic Dialogue and Grassroots Leadership components*	1998
			All interested national organizations	2000–2020

* See Civic Dialogue and Grassroots Leadership for types of organizations

Selected Recommendations with Time Tables and Implementation

Polis: An environment of behavior and accountability which sustains the common good

Task Force Recommendations	Strategies	Implementation	Target Location	Time Line
#1 National Association for the Southern Poor (NASP)	A. Develop videos and "how to" pamphlets for distribution to community groups. (Theme for materials: NASP's approach to community organizations' involvement in developing the polis.)	Don Anderson – National Association for the Southern Poor Kellogg AA male grantees. Assistance from Task Force members and their affiliated organizations	Atlanta, GA Washington, DC Cleveland, OH Chicago, IL	Jan.–Dec. 1997
	B. Develop "value" pamphlet which informs the ethic of the polis; test use of pamphlets in selected cities.		Atlanta, GA Washington, DC Chicago, IL	Jan.–Dec. 1997
	C. Enhance models and values materials based on experience and evaluation.			Jan.–Dec. 1998
	D. National Conference to share results and publicize the approach.		Los Angeles, CA	1999
	E1. Extend project to 10 other major metropolitan areas.		Kellogg AA Grantee Sites	2000
	E2. Convene 2nd Annual Conference.		Chicago, IL	2000
	F1. Establish regional offices in geographical areas of concentration.			2000 (announce at conference)
	F2. Continue Annual Conferences to perpetuate this concept/approval to polis development.			2000 (announce at conference)
	G. Continue expansion and evaluation of model.			2000–2012
	H. Determine continuation or discontinuation based on findings/recommendations.			2019–2026

Task Force Recommendations	Strategies	Implementation	Target Location	Time Line
#2 Establish the Domestic Service and Opportunity Corps	A. Planning Committee to collaborate with HBCUs and begin research on the concept.	Dr. Bobby Austin Dr. Karen Pitman HBCUs	TBD (suggest cities near HBCUs)	1997
	B. Develop strategies for collaboration and partnership with foundations and corporations.	Dr. Bobby Austin Dr. Karen Pitman HBCUs		1997
	C. Secure funding for Model Program and begin implementation.	Local volunteers		1998
	D. Begin using the National Association of Southern Poor model.			1999
	E. Expand and evaluate.			2001–2020
#3 Production of calendars/ planners designed especially for AA males	National approach to using a specially designed calendar/ planner for AA boys and their families. Calendars would note relevant holidays, ideas, and quotations reflective of AA culture and moral values, and tips on productive management of time.	1. Several think tank work groups, church organizations, national organizations (i.e., Masons, fraternities, etc.) to detail and design the concept and seek funding.		1996
		2. Consult with the National Black Child Development Institute (currently produces a calendar) and produce and distribute calendars.		1997
		3. Continue publishing and distributing calendars.		1998–2020

Task Force Recommenda-tions	Strategies	Implementation	Target Location	Time Line
#4 Youth Camps	A. Establish youth camps in at least four major regions of the U.S. for the purpose of teaching values, environ-mental education, conflict management/life skills, and information technology as a means of creating a non-violent and creative com-munity. Discontinued mili-tary bases an option for the "residential academies" that could operate either year-round or during summer vacation.	Dr. Samuel Proctor be empowered to establish and con-vene representatives from the Task Force to explore this idea, develop the propos-al, and market to both public and pri-vate sectors.		1997–2000
	B. Funds and location(s) iden-tified and secured.			1997–2000
	C. Secure and train staff.			1998
	D. Open and operate first Unit.			1998
	E. Expand incrementally to remaining three regions of the nation.			2000–2020
#5 Citizenship Schools	A. Convey to the Children's Defense Fund the interest of the Kellogg Task Force in assisting the Children's Crusade toward greater national success.	Dr. Bobby Austin		1996–1997
	B. Request that all organiza-tions represented on the Task Force assist in the implementation. Task Force Representatives			1996-2020

NOTES

1. In Howard Brotz, *African-American Social and Political Thought,*
   1850–1920 (New Brunswick, Maine: Transaction, 1992), 312–13.
2. Catalog of the exhibition (Philadelphia: Afro-American Historical and
   Cultural Museum, 1991), 16.
3. Catalog of the exhibition (African-American Family History Association,
   10.
4. John S. Mbiti, *African Religions and Philosophy* (Anchor Books, 1970)
   P.4C 44.
5. U.S. Census Bureau, *1990 Census: General Population Characteristics of
   the United States* (Washington, D.C.: Government Printing Office, 1992).
6. National Center for Health Statistics, Health, United States, 1993
   (Washington, D.C.: Government Printing Office, 1994).
7. Robert L. Green, *Improving African-American Family Life and the
   Education of the African-American Child* (Cleveland: Cleveland State
   University Urban Research Center, 1993).
8. U.S. Census, 1994. *Statistical Abstract of the United States,* 1994.
9. Green, et al., 1991; National Center for Educational Statistics, 1994
10. Green, Robert L. and Wright, Denise L. (Editor). 1985. *Metropolitan
    Desegregation.* New York: Prenum Press.
11. U.S. Census, 1992.
12. Green, Robert L. and Wright, Denise L., 1992. *African-American Males:
    a Demographic Study and Analysis.* Battlel Creek: Kellogg Foundation.
13. Green, Robert L. and Wright, Denise L., 1977, *The Urban Challenge—
    Poverty and Race.* Chicago: Follett Publishing.
14. Walter Lippmann, "The World Outside and the Pictures in Our Heads,"
    in *Images of Man: The Classic Tradition in Sociological Thinking,* ed. C.
    Wright Mills (New York: Braziller, 1960), 38. Lippmann provides some
    understanding of the sometimes perplexing situation all people are faced
    with in attempting to understand the world outside of themselves. He
    says, "For the most part, we do not foresee and then define. We define
    first, and then see. In the great blooming, buzzing confusion of the outer
    world, we pick up what our culture has already defined for us, and we
    tend to perceive that which we have picked out in the form stereotyped
    for us by our culture."
15. James MacGregor Burns, *Leadership* (New York: Harper, 1975), 36.
16. In Brotz, op. cit., 537.
17. In Brotz, op. cit., 217.

18. United Nations Human Development Programme, *Human Development Report* (New York: Oxford University Press, 1995).
19. Samuel D. Proctor, "The Concept for Communities and Youth Development: Community or Chaos" (speech delivered to the National Task Force on African-American Men and Boys, the Martin Luther King, Jr., Center for Non Violent Social Change, Atlanta, Ga., March 8, 1995).
20. W. E. B. DuBois, "In Battle for Peace, Masses and Mainstream," 1952, 154–55; quoted in Harold Cruse, *The Crisis of the Negro Intellectual* (New York: William Morrow, 1967), 334–35.
21. Pitirim A. Sorokin, "The Powers of Creative Unselfish Love," in *New Knowledge in Human Values*, ed. Abraham H. Maslow (New York: Harper, 1959), 3.
22. Ibid.
23. Bill Broadway, "Uncommon Prayer: Conversations with God Chronicles the Hopes and Despairs Reflected in Two Centuries of Devotions by African- Americans," *Washington Post*, 17 December 1994, sec D, p. 7.
24. Ibid.
25. Mbiti, op. cit., 141.
26. *National Center for Nonprofit Boards*, November-December, 1992, pages 4-5.
27. Robert N. Bellah et al., *Habits of the Heart: Individualism and Commitment in American Life* (New York: Harper, 1985), 285.
28. James Baldwin, "Everybody's Protest Novel," in *Notes of a Native Son* (New York: Beacon Press, 1955), 20.
29. Herbert Blumer, "Race Prejudice as a Sense of Group Position," in *Race Relations, Problems and Theory*, ed. Jitsuichi Masuoka and Preston Valien (Chapel Hill: University of North Carolina Press, 1955), 221–27.
30. George Gerbner, "Media Culture and the Image of African-American Men" (speech delivered to the National Task Force on African-American Men and Boys, Fisk University, Nashville, Tenn., October 22, 1994).
31. Ibid.
32. Ibid.
33. Harry Boyte, "Citizenship and Young African-Americans" (speech delivered to the National Task Force on African-American Men and Boys, the Martin Luther King, Jr., Center for Non-Violent Social Change, Atlanta, Ga., March 1995).
34. *Urban Family, the Magazine of Hope and Progress* (John M. Perkins Foundation for Reconciliation and Development, Pasadena, CA) 2, no. 1 (Spring 1993), 12.
35. Boyte, op. cit.
36. Hampton's Neighborhood College; prepared by Joyce Smith
37. Bobby W. Austin, ed., *What a Piece of Work Is Man!* (Battle Creek, Mich.: W. K. Kellogg Foundation, 1992), 22.
38. Parker Palmer "Leading from Within: Reflection on Spirituality and Leadership" (speech delivered at the Annual Celebration Dinner of the Indian Office for Campus Ministries, March 1990), 4.
39. Frances Moore Lappé, *Rediscovering America's Values* (New York: Ballantine Books, 1991), 252.

40. Michael H. Shuman, "Reclaiming the Inner City Through Political, Economic, and Ecological Self-Reliance" (commissioned paper for the W. K. Kellogg Foundation, 1955).

41. George E. Ayers, "Academic Imperatives: Parent Participation in Education Reform" (unpublished manuscript).

42. Richard J. Barnet and Ronald E. Muller, *Global Reach—The Power of the Multinational Corporations*

43. *Three Realities: Minority Life in the U.S.* A Report of the Business Higher Education Forum, June 1990, 19.

44. Gar Alperovitz argues that "distribution of income has worsened, step by step (as it is doing now) throughout most of the 20th century—except when interrupted by significant war, postwar boom, or depression collapse." "The Era of Fundamental Stalemate . . . and the Possibility of a Long 'Reconstructive' Revolution in America" (unpublished paper, 1992).

45. Kevin Phillips, *The Politics of Rich and Poor* (New York: Random House, 1990), 13, chart 2.

46. Paul Krugman, "The Right, the Rich, and the Facts," *The American Prospect* 11 (Fall 1992): 22

47. Ibid., 24–25.

48. James Head and Kelly Mogle, "Race, Poverty, and Lending," *X Clearinghouse Review* (1993), 358–62.

49. Ibid., 362.

50. 12 U.S.C. Sections 2901–2906.

51. Virginia M. Mayer, Maria Sampanes, and James Carras, Local Officials' Guide to the Community Reinvestment Act (Washington, D.C.: National League of Cities, 1991). See also Anthony D. Taibi, "Banking, Finance, and Community Economic Empowerment: Structural Economic Theory, Procedural Civil Rights, and Substantive Racial Justice," *Harvard Law Review* 107 (1994), 1463.

52. Conference speech, 1994 (cited in Staughton Lynd, forthcoming piece in Social Policy).

53. For further information, contact Working Capital, 99 Bishop Allen Drive, Cambridge, MA 02139, 617/576–8620.

54. David Skidmore, "Clinton Signs Measure Aimed at Spurring Credit in Poor Areas," *Boston Globe*, 24 September 1994, p. 63.

55. 12 U.S.C. Section 4701.

56. Skidmore, op. cit.

57. Anthony Ellsworth Scoville, "A Proposal for a Commission on the Investment of Social Security Trust Funds" (unpublished paper, 1992), 3.

58. Ibid., 3, 8.

59. Norm G. Kurland and Michael D. Greany, "The Third Way: America's True Legacy to the New Republics," in *Curing World Poverty: The New Role of Property*, ed. John H. Miller (St. Louis: Social Justice Review, 1994) 269–80.

60. Robert D. Putnam, "The Prosperous Community: Social Capital and Public Life," *The American Prospect* (Spring 1993), 36.

61. Ibid.

62. Ibid., 37.

63. Contact the Institute for Policy Studies, 1601 Connecticut Avenue, N.W., Washington, D.C. 20009, for the full text of Michael Shuman's paper, "Reclaiming the Inner City Through Political, Economic, and Ecological Self-Reliance."

64. Behnke and Associates, Inc.; Cuyahoga, Ohio, Metropolitan Housing Authority; Chicago Tribune/Steve Layton.

65. John L. McKnight and John P. Krutzman, *Mapping Community Capacity* (Evanston, IL: Northwestern University Center for Urban Affairs and Policy Research), 1–3.

66. Douglas Massey and Nancy Denton, *American Apartheid: Segregation and the Making of the Underclass*

67. Benjamin Barber, *Strong Democracy: Participatory Politics for a New Age*: University of California Press, 1984).

68. Ibid.

69. Barry Weisberg, "Megacity Security and Social Development: A Challenge for the World Summit for Social Development," Countdown to Istanbul *Forum* (February 1995), 10.

70. Ibid., 11.

71. Olivier DéGeorges (speech delivered at the International Forum on Urban Insecurity, University of Illinois at Chicago, September 1995), 6.

72. Ibid., 7.

73. Herbert J. Ganz, "Fitting the Poor into the Economy," *Forum* (October 1995).

74. Sidney M. Wilhelm, *Who Needs the Negro?* (Cambridge, Mass.: Schenkman, 1970). Quoted in Jeremy Rifkin and Jeremy P. Tarcher, *The End of Work* (New York: Putnam, 1995), 77.

75. *Juvenile Offenders and Victims: A National Report* (Washington, D.C.: U.S. Department of Justice, Office of Juvenile Justice and Delinquency Prevention), 104.

76. Robert Putnam, "What Makes Democracy Work in Civic Infrastructure," *National Civic Review* (Spring 1993), 106.

77. J. W. Gough, in *Second Treatise on Government* by John Locke (New York: Macmillan, 1956) xxxv.

78. Ralph Waldo Emerson, Essays (New York: Hurst & Company), 112.

79. James O'Toole, *The Executive's Compass* (New York: Oxford University Press, 1993), 23.

80. Brotz, op. cit., p. 382.

81. Jay Rosen, "Public Journalism: First Principles" in *Public Journalism: Theory and Practice*, ed Jay Rosen and Davis Merrit, Jr. (Occasional Paper of the Kettering Foundation, 1994), 6.

82. In Brotz, op. cit., 319.

83. Ibid, 316.

INDEX

Violence, 37, 101-102, 175
  in France, 162-163
  global context of, 159-169
  marketability, 74
  at Paradise at Parkside, 125-126

W

Washington, Booker T., 87, 172
Washington, D.C., 123-128, 132-133
Washington, James Melvin, 53, 60
Watson, Bernard, 17
Watson, Robert L., 17
Weisberg, Barry, 159-162
West, Cornell, 140
Whole system, 39-41, 170
Wilder, Douglas, 33
Wilhelm, Sidney M., 166
Wilson, Ernest J., 50
Wingspread Conference, 182

W.K. Kellogg Foundation. *See*
  Kellogg Foundation
Work group, 42
Working Capital, 109
Wright, Steven, 61
Wynn, Cordell, 17

Y

Young, Andrew, 15, 170, 199
Young People on the Rise, 127
Youth, 159-169
Youth commissions, 90
Youth policy, 117
Youth Policy Institute, 132
YouthBuild, 151
Ypsilanti, Michigan, 201